What Will I Do With
All Those Courgettes?

Elaine Borish, an American living in London, was born in New York City. She holds degrees from Rutgers, Boston University, and Northeastern University and has taught at universities in New England. In old England, she has lectured in English and American literature at Morley College in London. Her numerous articles have appeared in leading newspapers and magazines.

Also by Elaine Borish

A Legacy of Names
Literary Lodgings
Novel Cuisine
This Book Is Unpublishable!

Elaine Borish

What Will I Do With All Those Courgettes?

Fidelio Press

Telluride · London

Dedicated to the avid gardener who keeps me supplied with
copious courgettes and a zillion zucchini

Published by
Fidelio Press, Inc.
129 Aldasoro Road
Telluride CO 81435
USA

Reprinted 2005
Reprinted 2006
Reprinted 2007
Reprinted 2008

Produced by Braiswick at By Design
http://www.braiswick.com

Printed in Finland

Cover design by Kate Chitham

PREFACE

Make no mistake, courgettes or zucchini mean exactly the same thing. I use the words interchangeably.

Whether you call them courgettes (as the English and French do) or zucchini (as do Americans and Italians), gardens can yield enormous amounts, especially for people involved in growing their own organic food. This book was inspired by two stories:

I asked Larry what he does with the vast quantities of the zucchini crop I had just seen him harvest. "Well," he replied unblinking, "I put them into a large brown paper bag, go to a neighbor's house and place them on the doorstep. Then I ring the doorbell—and run like hell!"

Kathy, an avid gardener in a neighborhood allotment in North London, recalls her growing-up days in Iowa when one did not dare to leave the car door unlocked in the summertime. Anyone who failed to use a key took the risk of returning to find the car filled with zucchini.

The great thing about an abundant crop is the infinite variety of ways in which to use it. No need to rack your brain for ideas for cooking them. Here are some one hundred fifty easy-to-prepare and good recipes for consuming the entire crop. They must be easy because I've made them—and good because Marty helps me eat them.

Even if you do not have a garden, you can grow courgettes at home in a tub on the balcony or in some outdoor space. Freshly picked when they are still small, courgettes are remarkably good. Be warned, you may develop a passion for this wonderful and versatile vegetable.

And remember, I use the words for this versatile vegetable—courgette or zucchini—interchangeably. Also, my favorite word in giving recipes is "about" because preparation should be easy and fun, and undue concern for exactness should not outweigh your own logical application.

Courgette

Zucchini

Contents

CASSEROLES

MAIN COURSES

ACCOMPANIMENTS

Soups

Favorite Courgette Soup

The first courgette soup I ever made, equally good hot or cold, remains a favorite because it is easy to make as well as delicious—and the ingredients keep guests guessing. Make double or triple quantities, as this soup freezes well.

**3 medium courgettes (about 1 lb or 450 g), cut into
thick slices
24 fl oz (3 cups or 700 ml) chicken stock
1 medium onion, sliced
¼ teaspoon oregano
¼ teaspoon rosemary
salt and pepper, to taste**

1. Place all the ingredients into a large pot and bring to a boil. Reduce heat, cover and simmer for about 15-20 minutes.
2. Blend in a food processor until smooth. Add more water if necessary. Reheat when ready to serve. Or chill and serve cold.

6 servings

2

Zucchini Potato Soup

Serve hot in winter or chilled in summer.

2 medium potatoes, peeled and sliced
2 cans chicken broth (about 28 oz or 800 ml)
2 medium zucchini, sliced
3-4 spring onions, sliced
1 medium onion, sliced
2 tablespoons butter
salt and pepper to taste
2 teaspoons thyme, or to taste

1. Cook potatoes in chicken broth until almost tender. Add sliced zucchini and cook until soft.
2. Sauté spring onions and onions in butter over low heat until transparent.
3. Add salt and pepper and thyme. Purée all ingredients in a food processor until smooth.
4. Serve with a dollop of yogurt or sour cream.

Serves 6-8

Courgette and Mint Soup

Here's another soup that may be served either hot or cold.

2 oz (50 g) butter
2 medium onions, chopped
2 lbs (900 g) courgettes, chopped in chunks
24 oz (3 cups or 700 ml) chicken stock
2 handfuls of mint leaves
salt
freshly ground black pepper

1. In a large pot, melt the butter and add the chopped onions. Sauté over low heat until the onions are soft and translucent, about 10 minutes. Add the courgettes and cook for an additional 5 minutes.
2. Add the chicken stock and 1 handful of mint leaves.
3. Cover and simmer for 30 minutes. Cool.
4. Blend the contents in a food processor together with the remaining handful of mint leaves.
5. Add more water if needed and season with salt and pepper.

Serves 6

Courgette Soup with Mint

Similar to the previous recipe, this courgette-and-mint soup variation includes potato and yields a thick texture and delectable flavor.

2 oz (50 g) butter
1 bunch of spring
  onions
1 garlic clove, finely
  chopped
1 medium potato, cut
  into cubes
salt and pepper
2 large courgettes, grated
24 fl oz (3 cups or

700 ml)
chicken or vegetable
  stock
7 fl oz (200 ml) milk
handful of mint leaves
handful of flat leaf
  parsley
Parmesan cheese

1. Melt the butter in a pot and add sliced spring onions and chopped garlic. Cook and stir for about five minutes, until soft but not brown.
2. Add the potato cubes and cook for a few minutes more. Add salt and pepper to taste.
3. Add the grated courgettes and continue cooking for another few minutes.
4. Add stock and simmer for five minutes, or until potato is tender.
5. Add milk, mint, and parsley. Bring to a boil. Then blend in a food processor.
6. Return to pot and reheat. Adjust seasonings and serve with grated Parmesan cheese.

Serves 6

Zucchini Watercress Soup

Here's another delicious variation that makes a perfect beginner to almost any dinner.

4 tablespoons butter
2 medium onions, chopped
24 fl oz (3 cups or 700 ml) chicken stock
5-6 medium zucchini (2 lbs or nearly 1 kg), cut into small pieces
1 large bunch watercress (about 4 loosely-packed cups   or 100 g)
3 tablespoons fresh lemon juice
salt and pepper, to taste

1. Melt butter, add onions, and cook in a large covered pot over low heat until onions are soft and golden (about 15-20 minutes).
2. Add chicken stock and bring to a boil. Add zucchini and simmer, covered, until zucchini are tender (about 20 minutes).
3. Add watercress. Remove pot from heat, cover, and allow to stand for 5 minutes.
4. Purée soup in food processor until smooth.
5. Return to pot and add lemon juice. Season with salt and pepper.
6. Add additional stock, if necessary, to obtain desired consistency. Heat when ready to serve.

Serves 6

Courgette and Dill Soup

You may want to add more stock (up to another pint) for a thinner consistency, but be cautious with the amount of dill as it is a strong herb.

**1 medium onion, chopped
2 oz (50 g) butter
1 large courgette, peeled and sliced
2 teaspoons flour
35 fl oz (4¼ cups or 1 litre) stock
salt and pepper to taste
2 egg yolks
2 tablespoons heavy or double cream
extra pat of butter
dill weed**

1. Sauté the onion in butter in a large pot for 5 minutes. Add the sliced courgettes, cover and cook for another 5 minutes, until vegetables are golden.
2. Sprinkle in the flour and stir. Add about half the liquid and simmer until courgette is just cooked.
3. Purée in a blender or food processor. Return to pot and add the remaining stock and the salt and pepper. Reheat.
4. In a bowl, beat together the egg yolks and cream and pour a ladleful of the soup into the egg mixture. Blend it all together and pour the mixture back into the pot. Stir over a low heat just to bind the soup smoothly.
5. Add the pat of butter. Sprinkle with chopped dill weed and serve.

Serves 6-8

Tomato-Zucchini Soup

Another soup that is good either hot or cold.

2 tablespoons olive oil
2 medium onions, sliced
5-6 small zucchini, sliced
35 fl oz (4¼ cups or 1 litre) chicken broth
2 large tomatoes, skinned and chopped
1 small bunch parsley, finely chopped
1 tablespoon chopped chives
1 teaspoon salt
pinch of sugar
4-5 chopped fresh basil leaves or ½ teaspoon dried basil
2 teaspoons lemon juice

1. In a large pot, heat the oil and add the onion and zucchini. Cover and cook slowly for 10 minutes.
2. Add the chicken broth and simmer for an additional 20 minutes.
3. Remove zucchini and onions from broth and purée together with tomatoes in a blender or food processor. Return the zucchini mixture to pot and add the rest of the ingredients. Cook 5 minutes more. Serve hot or cold.

Serves 8

Courgette and Fennel Soup

The fennel imparts a mild and refreshing aniseed flavor to this soup, which you can make ahead of time and reheat when needed.

3 oz (80 g) butter
l large onion, chopped
1 lb (450 g) courgettes, sliced
1 lb (450 g) leaves of fennel bulb, cut into small pieces
5 fl oz (150 ml) dry sherry
½ teaspoon salt
freshly ground black pepper
½ teaspoon sugar
32-35 fl oz (4-4¼ cups or 900 ml-1 litre) stock

1. Melt the butter in a pot and add chopped onions. Sauté slowly until golden.
2. Add courgettes and fennel together with sherry, salt and pepper, and sugar.
3. Pour in stock. Cover and simmer on low heat for 40-45 minutes.
4. Liquidize in a food processor.
5. Adjust seasonings and add more water or stock as needed.
6. Reheat just before serving.

Serves 8-10

Zucchini Pesto Soup

This soup is good in the summertime, served warm rather than hot, together with good, fresh bread.

3 tablespoons olive oil
2 medium onions, chopped
4 small zucchini (about 1½ lbs or 700 g) cut in ½-inch (1.2 cm) cubes
3 medium potatoes, peeled and cut in 1-inch (2.5 cm) cubes
16 fl oz (2 cups or 450 ml) chicken stock
32 fl oz (4 cups or 900 ml) water
2 oz (50 g) spaghetti broken into 1-inch (2.5 cm) pieces
salt and pepper to taste
3 large cloves garlic, chopped
2 handfuls basil leaves
1 handful parsley leaves
1 tablespoon pine nuts (optional)
2 oz (50 g) grated Parmesan cheese
2-3 tablespoons olive oil

1. Heat the 3 tablespoons olive oil in a large pot over medium heat. Add onions and cook for about 15 minutes until golden. Add the zucchini and potatoes and cook, continuing to stir occasionally, for another 10 minutes.
2. Add the stock and water. Increase the heat to medium-high to reach boiling point. Then reduce heat and simmer, uncovered, for 30 minutes.
3. Add the spaghetti and the salt and pepper. Simmer about 10 minutes, until the spaghetti is cooked.

4. Blend the garlic, basil and parsley (and pine nuts, if used) in a food processor. Add the cheese and blend it in. While processing, slowly stream in the olive oil until the mixture forms a thick paste. Add salt and pepper to taste. Turn the pesto out into a large bowl.
5. Ladle about 1 cup of the soup into the pesto and combine, stirring briskly. Return this mixture to the soup remaining in the pot and mix it all together. Remove from the heat, cover, and allow to stand for 5 minutes. Adjust seasonings.
6. Sprinkle additional cheese into each bowl of soup and serve.

6-8 servings

Curry Zucchini Soup

This is another soup that may be eaten hot or cold, winter or summer—and freezes well.

3 or 4 medium zucchini, sliced
1 medium onion, chopped
2 oz (¼ cup or 50 g) rice
20 oz (2½ cups or 600 ml) chicken stock
1 teaspoon salt
1 teaspoon curry powder
1 teaspoon mustard
4-8 oz (½-1 cup or 100-225 g) yogurt

1. Place zucchini, onion, rice, chicken stock, and salt in a large pot.
2. Add water, if necessary, to cover zucchini and simmer until zucchini are tender, about 15 minutes.
3. Blend in a food processor together with curry powder, mustard, and yogurt.

Serves 8

Sliced Zucchini Soup

Here is another way to use zucchini—with a crunch—in soup.

1 large onion, chopped
celery stalk, chopped
2 tablespoons olive oil
8 oz (1 cup or 225 g) raw rice
4 tomatoes, peeled, seeded, and chopped
48 fl oz (6 cups or approximately 1.4 litres) chicken or
   beef broth
4 small zucchini
5 tablespoons minced fresh chives or parsley
salt and freshly ground black pepper
grated Parmesan cheese

1. Sauté coarsely-chopped onion and celery in olive oil until onions
   turn golden.
2. Add rice and cook another 3 minutes, stirring frequently.
3. Add tomatoes and broth. Cook over medium heat until rice is
   just tender.
4. Add thinly sliced zucchini and the chives or parsley and cook
   covered for about 5 minutes. (Add more water, if needed.) The
   zucchini should still be crisp. Season with salt and pepper to
   taste.
5. Serve hot with grated Parmesan cheese on the side.

Serves 8-10

Ratatouille Soup

A hearty soup that is thick and textured.

1 ½ tablespoons olive oil
1 large onion, chopped
1 green pepper, chopped
2 cloves garlic, chopped
1 ½ lbs (700 g) aubergine (eggplant) peeled and cut into
   ¼-inch (.6 cm) cubes
2 1-lb (450 g) tins tomatoes, undrained, chopped
3-4 medium-large zucchini, unpeeled
32 fl oz (4 cups or 900 ml) water or stock (vegetable or
   chicken)
1 bay leaf
1 ¼ teaspoons dried basil
1 ¼ teaspoons dried oregano
salt and pepper to taste
6 oz (175 g) of any very small pasta

1. Heat oil in a large soup pot. Add onions, green pepper, and garlic. Cook about 5 minutes, until tender.
2. Add cubed aubergine (eggplant). Cook 5 minutes, stirring frequently and adding water if necessary to prevent sticking.
3. Cut zucchini in half lengthwise, then into ¼-inch (.6 cm) slices. Add water or stock and spices. Bring to a boil, then reduce to low heat, and cover and cook for 45 minutes.
4. Add pasta, cover and cook for 10 minutes.
5. Discard bay leaf and serve.

8 servings

Minestrone

The beans, pasta, and chunky vegetables can make this hearty soup a meal when served with hot crusty bread.

8 oz (225 g) dried haricot beans
2 tablespoons olive oil
1 medium onion, chopped
3-4 cloves garlic, minced
1 stalk celery, finely chopped
1 large carrot, diced
1 small can tomatoes
34 fl oz (about 4¼ cups or 1 litre) vegetable stock
4 oz (100 g) small fine pasta such as conchigliette
1 zucchini, cubed or thinly sliced
salt and freshly ground pepper
4 tablespoons finely chopped parsley
2 oz (50 g) grated Parmesan cheese

1. Soak the beans in cold water overnight. On the following day, drain and put them in a saucepan, covering them with fresh water. Simmer until nearly tender, about 20 minutes.
2. Heat the olive oil in a pot and add the onion, garlic, celery and carrot. Cover pot and simmer for about 10 minutes, stirring occasionally. Add the tomatoes (broken up) and stock. Cover and simmer for 1 hour.
3. Mix in the beans and add the pasta and zucchini. Add salt to taste and grind in some pepper. Add more boiling stock as necessary. Cook until pasta is tender. Sprinkle with parsley and Parmesan cheese and serve.

Serves 8-10

Spring Vegetable Soup

Here is another flavorful and colorful soup to add to your easy weekday repertory. Serve with ciabatta or other rustic bread.

2 tablespoons olive oil
1 small onion, finely chopped
2 garlic cloves, finely chopped
1 medium potato, diced
20 fl oz (2½ cups or 600 ml) vegetable or chicken stock
1 carrot, sliced diagonally (or turnip)
4 oz (110 g) curly kale (or spring greens)
2 oz (50 g) fresh or frozen peas
2 small courgettes, sliced
salt and pepper
chili oil (optional)
fresh flat-leaf parsley, coarsely chopped

1. Heat oil in a large pot and cook the onion, garlic and potato in it for 3-4 minutes, stirring occasionally, until softened.
2. Add stock and simmer for 5 minutes. Add carrots and continue cooking for 3 minutes. Then add kale, peas, and courgettes. Season and cook for another 2-3 minutes.
3. For a spicy flavor, add a few drops of chili oil. Serve, garnished with parsley.

Serves 4

Thai Soup with Cellophane Noodles

*This easy-to-prepare soup will be even easier if you are able to
buy small bundles of cellophane or rice noodles, rather than
trying to cut some off from a big bundle.*

small bundle cellophane or mung bean noodles (or rice
    noodles), about 2 oz (50 g)
40 fl oz (5 cups or 1200 ml) chicken or vegetable stock
1 medium-large onion, thinly sliced
2-3 cloves garlic, minced
4-6 mushrooms, thinly sliced
2 small zucchini, thinly sliced
1 tablespoon soy sauce
salt and pepper

1. Soak noodles in hot water until softened, and then cut them
   into short lengths.
2. Bring stock to a boil and add onion, garlic, and the drained
   and cut noodles. Cook until noodles are swollen and soft, about
   10 minutes.
3. Add the mushrooms, zucchini, and soy sauce and cook until
   just tender but still crunchy, about 5 minutes. Add salt and
   pepper to taste and serve hot right away.

Serves 8-10

Zucchini Bisque

I relented on the cholesterol count for this recipe, which is made with butter and cream. (But skimmed milk may be substituted for the cream.)

1 medium onion, chopped
4 oz (100 g) butter
4-5 zucchini (about 1½ lbs or 700 g), shredded
24 fl oz (3 cups or 700 ml) chicken stock
1 teaspoon dried basil
½ teaspoon nutmeg
1 teaspoon salt
freshly ground black pepper
8 fl oz (1 cup or 240 ml) heavy cream

1. Melt butter in large pot and add chopped onion. Sauté until soft and golden.
2. Add shredded zucchini and chicken stock to the onion.
3. Cover pot and simmer for 15 minutes.
4. Purée contents, adding basil, nutmeg, salt and pepper.
5. Add cream and mix well. Serve hot or cold.

6-7 servings

Gazpacho

There are many variations of this refreshing summertime soup that comes from Spain. Why not add a raw cubed courgette to vary this traditional cold soup?

3 large tomatoes, peeled
1 clove garlic
1 medium onion, sliced
1 green pepper, seeded
1 cucumber, sliced (or half of a large one)
1 stalk celery
salt
½ teaspoon black pepper
5 tablespoons red wine vinegar
4 tablespoons olive oil
32 oz (4 cups or 900 ml) tomato juice

Garnish:
8 oz (225 g) bread cubes or croutons
1 onion, chopped
1 green pepper, chopped
1 courgette, peeled and cubed

1. Purée tomatoes, garlic, onion, pepper, cucumber and celery in a food processor. Combine all ingredients in a large bowl, adding salt and pepper, wine vinegar, olive oil and tomato juice.
2. Chill overnight and serve ice cold.
3. Just before serving, add any or all garnish ingredients— bread cubes, onion, green pepper, and courgette—or serve garnish ingredients separately for diners to help themselves.

Serves 8

19

Mexican Courgette Blossom Soup

Save blossoms from your courgette plants and store them in freezer until you accumulate enough to make this unusual, conversation-producing soup. For a dinner party, you will need to double this recipe, but the effort will undoubtedly double the party conversation, as you discuss the exotic secret ingredient. Note that since each flower weighs about ½ oz or 10 grams, you will need about 16 to 20 flowers.

32 fl oz (4 cups or 900 ml) chicken stock
4 oz (100 g) corn kernels, fresh or frozen
1 oz (25 g) butter
½ onion, finely chopped
1 clove garlic, crushed
1 tablespoon tomato purée
1 tablespoon chopped fresh coriander
2 oz (50 g) mushrooms, (about 6 medium-large
  mushrooms), sliced
8 oz (225 g) courgette blossoms
freshly ground pepper to taste
2 tablespoons shredded cheese

1. Put the stock in a saucepan and bring to a boil. Add the corn and cook for 5 minutes.
2. Heat the butter in a frying pan and sauté the onion and garlic until limp. Add tomato purée, coriander, mushrooms and broken-up blossoms and sauté for a further 5 minutes. Sprinkle in a few grinds of pepper.
3. Add this mixture to the stock and serve hot, garnished with shredded cheese.

Serves 4

Salads

Chunky Salad with Zucchini

This is easy to prepare because everything—the amounts are not very crucial—is just mixed together to make a colorful salad. Other raw vegetables (such as broccoli or cauliflower) may be added.

1 small onion, chopped
½ green pepper, chopped
½ sweet red pepper, chopped
3-4 tomatoes, chopped
20 small stuffed green olives, sliced
20 small pitted black olives, sliced
8-10 mushrooms, sliced
1 carrot, thinly sliced
1 zucchini (8 oz or 225 g), unpeeled and cut into chunks
1 yellow zucchini or squash (8 oz or 225 g), cut into
   chunks
1 small cucumber or half a large one (8 oz or 225 g), cut
   in half lengthwise, then thinly sliced
2 tablespoons dried parsley flakes
½ teaspoon dried dill weed
¼ teaspoon garlic powder
2-3 fl oz (about ¼ cup or 75 ml) Italian dressing

1. Combine all ingredients in a large bowl and mix well.
2. Cover and chill, mixing several times before it is ready to be
    used.

Serves 8

Courgette and Radicchio Salad

Use any good vinaigrette dressing, or the recipe below.

6 tablespoons vinaigrette dressing
1 clove garlic, minced
1 medium courgette, thinly sliced
1 head radicchio
12-16 small pitted black olives
1 tablespoon pine nuts (pignoli)
salt and freshly ground black pepper

1. Place vinaigrette, garlic, and sliced courgettes in a salad bowl and toss. Allow to stand for a half hour while courgettes absorb the flavor of the dressing.
2. Cut radicchio leaves into pieces and add to salad bowl together with black olives and pine nuts.
3. Season with salt and pepper. Toss with dressing before serving.

Serves 4-6

Dressing:
1 teaspoon French mustard
5 fl oz (150 ml) oil
4 tablespoons wine vinegar
salt and freshly ground black pepper
sugar to taste

1. Combine all ingredients in a small jar and cover tightly.
2. Mix well by shaking the jar, thoroughly blending together the ingredients.

Raw Courgette Salad in Radicchio Cups

If radicchio is unavailable, substitute a red leaf lettuce such as frilly-edged Lollo Rosso to make an attractive-looking salad.

1 large courgette, grated
1 carrot, grated
2-3 tablespoons French dressing
4 large radicchio leaves

1. Toss grated courgettes and grated carrots in a good, herbed French dressing.
2. Chill and serve in radicchio cups.

Serves 4

Raw Zucchini and Mushroom Salad

Requires no cooking—perfect on a hot summer day.

1 large zucchini, about 9 oz (250 g), sliced
6 oz (175 g) firm white mushrooms, sliced

Dressing:
4 tablespoons sunflower oil
2 tablespoons walnut or hazelnut oil
3 tablespoons lemon juice
¼ teaspoon pepper
1 teaspoon honey
1 clove garlic, crushed
1 tablespoon finely chopped spring onions or chives
2 tablespoons freshly chopped parsley

1. Place the sliced zucchini in a salad bowl together with the sliced mushrooms.
2. Whisk together all the dressing ingredients.
3. Toss gently and serve.

Serves 4-6

Raw Zucchini Julienne Salad

Substitute fresh basil, if you have it, to make the salad even more delicious.

4 small zucchini
1 spring onion, finely chopped
4-5 tablespoons olive oil
6 tablespoons red wine vinegar
½ teaspoon oregano
½ teaspoon basil
salt and pepper

Optional extras:
clove of garlic, crushed
red onion, minced
finely chopped parsley
thinly sliced mushrooms

1. Cut small zucchini into thin lengthwise slices, then cut thinly widthwise to make julienne strips. Place in a bowl.
2. Add all other ingredients, mix gently, and chill in refrigerator until cold.

Serves 4

Courgette and Chive Salad

If chives are unavailable, finely-cut spring onions may be substituted.

3 small courgettes (about 12 oz or 350 g)
1 tablespoon olive oil
juice of half a lemon
salt and freshly-ground black pepper
2 tablespoons chopped chives

1. Place the courgettes in a large pan of boiling water for about 3-5 minutes, just long enough to reduce the bitterness of the skin. Drain immediately in a colander and rinse in cold water to stop them cooking.
2. Cut courgettes into slices ½-inch (1.2 cm) thick and place them in a shallow serving dish.
3. Blend the oil, lemon juice, salt and pepper, and pour this dressing over the courgettes.
4. Add the chopped chives and mix thoroughly. Refrigerate to chill the salad before serving.

Serves 4

Mashed Zucchini Salad

Smaller zucchini, which do not have large seeds, will make a smoother mash for this exotic salad.

6-8 small zucchini (about 1½ lbs or 700 g)
juice of half a lemon
2 tablespoons olive oil
3 garlic cloves, crushed
1 teaspoon ground coriander
dash of pepper
salt, to taste
10 black olives, cut into halves

1. Boil zucchini until they are soft. Drain and press out excess water. Cut up with knife and then mash.
2. Add the other ingredients and mix all together. Serve cold.

Serves 6

Marinated Courgettes

This salad makes a good appetizer or main course accompaniment. It may also be kept in the refrigerator for a week and used to enliven other salads or sandwiches.

3 small courgettes (about 1 lb or 450 g)
2 tablespoons olive oil
4 garlic cloves, crushed
salt and freshly ground pepper, to taste
1 tablespoon chopped fresh mint or basil
1 tablespoon balsamic or red wine vinegar

1. Cut courgettes diagonally into oval-shaped slices.
2. Heat oil in a large pan, and sauté courgette slices with garlic until they are golden on both sides. Sprinkle with salt and pepper and more oil if necessary.
3. Drain fried slices on paper towels.
4. Place the courgette slices in a bowl and scatter over them the fresh herbs and vinegar.
5. Serve at room temperature.

Serves 4

Courgette Vinaigrette

I make this for fancy picnics and large barbecue parties.

2 lbs (1 kg) small courgettes, cut into ¼-inch (.6 cm) slices
1 small-medium red onion, chopped
1 teaspoon oregano or basil
2 oz (50 g) chopped parsley
6 fl oz (¾ cup or 180 ml) French dressing
1-2 cloves garlic, crushed

1. Cook courgettes in a large pot of boiling water for just 2 minutes. Drain immediately in a colander and rinse in cold water to stop the cooking process.
2. Place courgettes in a bowl and add onion, oregano and parsley.
3. Mix crushed garlic with the French dressing and pour over the courgettes.
4. Blend thoroughly and chill.

8 servings

Pasta Salad Sweet and Sour

Just add small bits of cooked chicken pieces if you would like to turn this into a main course salad.

1 can (15 oz or 425 g) pineapple chunks
6-8 oz (175-225 g) broccoli florets
12 oz spiral-shaped pasta, cooked (or other shape)
1 medium courgette, cubed
2 stalks celery, chopped
1-2 spring onions, chopped
½ sweet red pepper, chopped
chopped parsley

Dressing:
2 tablespoons pineapple juice
½ teaspoon garlic powder
1 tablespoon olive oil
3¼ fl oz (1/3 cup or 100 ml) white vine vinegar
2 tablespoons fresh lemon juice
2 tablespoons French mustard
2 tablespoons honey
½ teaspoon dried basil

1. Drain pineapple chunks saving 2 tablespoons of juice for dressing.
2. Combine all salad ingredients in a bowl.
3. Mix all dressing ingredients together. Toss the salad with the dressing.
4. Garnish with parsley.

Serves 10

Rice Salad with Zucchini and Peppers

This colorful and filling salad looks attractive and tastes good too.

1 lb (500 g) rice
28 fl oz (3½ cups or 800 ml) vegetable stock
½ teaspoon ground turmeric
½ teaspoon salt
2-3 small zucchini, thinly sliced
1 red pepper, chopped
1 green pepper, chopped
3 small onions, sliced into thin rings
5 oz (140 g) black olives
8 fl oz (1 cup or 240 ml) French dressing

1. In a large pot, combine rice with vegetable stock, turmeric and salt. Bring to a boil, then lower heat and simmer covered for 20 minutes.
2. Remove lid and allow steam to escape for 5 minutes. Then turn rice into a large bowl and allow to cool completely. Chill in covered bowl and set aside until needed.
3. Mix in the zucchini, peppers, onions, and olives. Add dressing. Toss and mix thoroughly.

Serves 8-10

Layered Vegetable Salad

This makes a good alternative to ordinary potato salad.

4-5 medium potatoes (about 1½ lbs or 700 g)
4 fl oz (½ cup or 100 ml) red wine vinegar
2 fl oz (¼ cup or 50 ml) olive oil
1 clove garlic, crushed
1 teaspoon basil
¼ teaspoon oregano
¼ teaspoon pepper
3 tablespoon spring onions, sliced
2 tablespoons chopped parsley
salt
2 large tomatoes, sliced
2 medium zucchini, shredded

1. Cook potatoes in boiling water until just tender (about 25 minutes).
2. Make the dressing by whisking together vinegar, oil, garlic, basil, oregano and pepper. Add onions, parsley and salt.
3. Slice the cooled potatoes ¼ inch (.6 cm) thick.
4. Layer half the potatoes, tomatoes and zucchini in a serving bowl and ladle half the dressing over the layer. Make another layer with the remaining vegetables and top with remaining dressing.
5. Cover. Chill before serving.

Serves 6-8

Pickled Zucchini

Why not? After all, pickled cucumbers were invented because a plentiful harvest allowed them to be kept for winter usage.

2 lbs (nearly 1 kg) small zucchini, about 1 inch (2.5 cm)   in diameter
12 oz (¾ lb or 350 g) small onions, sliced into thin rounds
2 oz (50 g) pickling salt
16 fl oz (2 cups or 450 ml) cider vinegar
8 oz (1 cup or 225 g) sugar
2 tablespoons yellow mustard seeds
1 tablespoon celery seeds
1 teaspoon ground turmeric

1. Slice zucchini into ¼ inch (.6 cm) rounds and place in a bowl together with the onion. Mix in the salt. Cover the vegetables with ice cubes and allow to stand for 2 hours. Drain well.
2. Combine vinegar, sugar, and spices in a saucepan and bring to a boil. Add vegetables and bring them slowly to a boil, stirring frequently. Reduce heat and simmer 5 minutes.
3. Ladle vegetables and liquid into warmed-up preserving jars with an airtight seal, packing vegetables loosely and leaving a ½ inch (1.2 cm) space at top. Close and secure jars with a good seal.
4. Store them in a cool, dry place for at least 3 weeks before using.

Makes about 3-4 pints

Courgette Chutney

This recipe will not only help to deplete your bumper crop, but will allow you to use bruised courgettes, as long as you cut away any spoiled or rotten parts. I freeze mine in small containers for convenient usage the year round.

2 lbs (1 kg) courgettes, chopped
3 lbs (1.5 kg) tomatoes, chopped
1½ lbs (700 g) onions, sliced
2 cloves garlic, chopped
20 fl oz (2½ cups or 600 ml) vinegar
1 teaspoon salt
1 teaspoon mustard
1 teaspoon red or cayenne pepper
1 tablespoon paprika
1 lb (450 g) brown sugar
4 oz (110 g) raisins

1. In a large pot, heat the courgettes, tomatoes, onions, and garlic with half the vinegar and simmer uncovered until vegetables are soft, about 30 minutes.
2. Add the rest of the vinegar and all the remaining ingredients. Simmer for about 1 hour, stirring occasionally to prevent sticking. It should be thick and reduced to a pulp, with no watery juices left. Pour into jars with airtight seal. Or freeze.

Yield: 5 lbs (2.5 kg)

Appetizers

Crudités with Vinaigrette

This healthy starter is a good choice for dinner parties and works well at finger buffets.

Vegetables:
zucchini, carrots, celery, cucumber cut into thin sticks
green, red, yellow peppers cut into strips
broccoli, cut into spears
cauliflower cut into small florets

Vinaigrette Dip:
1 teaspoon French (Dijon) mustard
5 oz (150 ml) oil
4 tablespoons wine vinegar
1 clove garlic, minced
salt
freshly ground black pepper

1. Arrange a selection of any of the crisp raw vegetables, as suggested above, on a serving platter.
2. Serve with a dip such as this vinaigrette, which can be made up and kept in a large container. Simply combine all the ingredients in a small jar, cover tightly, and shake well to mix thoroughly.

Zucchini Appetizer Salad

Another attractive salad variation that makes a good appetizer.

Salad:
8 small zucchini
lettuce leaves
2 medium tomatoes,
  peeled and chopped
½ small green pepper,
  chopped
3 tablespoons spring
  onions, finely chopped
1 tablespoon capers,
  chopped
1 tablespoon parsley,
  chopped

1 teaspoon basil
½ teaspoon oregano

Dressing:
4 fl oz (120 ml or ½
  cup) fresh lemon juice
4 fl oz (120 ml or ½
  cup) olive oil
1 large garlic clove,
  minced
salt and pepper

1. Make the dressing by combining ingredients in a jar which can be shaken to mix thoroughly. Set aside.
2. Steam whole unpeeled zucchini for about 3-4 minutes. Rinse in cold water to stop further cooking. Drain.
3. Cut each zucchini in half lengthwise and scoop out the pulp. Place the zucchini shells, cut sides up, in a flat dish. Pour half the dressing over them and allow to marinate in refrigerator for at least 4 hours.
4. When ready to serve, remove zucchini (discarding the marinade) and place them, cut side up, on lettuce leaves which have been arranged on a serving platter.
5. Mix salad ingredients with the other half of the dressing and pour into the hollow zucchini shells, allowing the dressing to spill over and around.

Serves 8

Carpaccio Courgettes

An elegant but easy appetizer to make when you have a glut from the garden.

3 small courgettes (about 1 lb or 450 g)
4 fl oz (120 ml) olive oil
1 tablespoon fresh lemon juice
salt and pepper, to taste
2 oz (50 g) Parmesan cheese

1. Cut the courgettes lengthwise into very thin slices with a sharp knife or a food processor. Arrange slightly overlapping slices on a serving platter.
2. Whisk together the oil, lemon juice, and salt and pepper in a small bowl. Trickle the mixture over the courgettes.
3. Strew thinly-shaved slices of cheese over the courgettes and serve.

4 servings

Courgette Paté

This excellent first course is enhanced by the tomato vinaigrette accompaniment, which simply blends ingredients together, and further enhanced when made a day ahead of time.

2 lbs (1 kg) courgettes, sliced
2 large onions, chopped
3 tablespoons olive oil
1 teaspoon cornstarch (or flour)
6 oz (175 g) fresh white breadcrumbs
1 tablespoon fresh basil leaves, cut up
1 tablespoon fresh tarragon
dash of nutmeg
salt and pepper to taste
3 eggs, beaten
butter

Tomato Vinaigrette Sauce (optional):
4 tomatoes
6 tablespoons olive oil
2 tablespoons red wine vinegar
salt and pepper

1. Heat oil in a large frying pan and sauté the courgettes and onions. When soft, add cornstarch and blend it all together in a food processor, not too smoothly.
2. Turn the mixture into a bowl. Add breadcrumbs, basil, tarragon, nutmeg, salt and pepper. Add beaten eggs and mix all together.
3. Put the mixture into a well-buttered paté or loaf tin, about 12 x 4 inches (30 x 12 cm).

41

4. Bake for 1 hour in a 350°F (180°C) oven.
5. Let cool and refrigerate until a half hour before ready to serve. Remove and slice the paté.
6. To make the vinaigrette, peel, remove seeds, and chop the tomatoes. Blend the ingredients together. Serve separately.

Serves 8

Ratatouille

This highly flavored Mediterranean vegetable stew is popular in French provincial cooking and may be eaten hot—or cold as an appetizer. Aubergines (eggplants) can be made less bitter by sprinkling with salt and allowing juices to drain away in a colander for 30 minutes.

4 tablespoons olive oil
1 large onion, chopped
4 large cloves garlic,
  minced
1 small aubergine
  (eggplant), peeled and
  cubed
2 medium green or red
  peppers, cut into strips
3 tablespoons red wine
1 bay leaf
1 teaspoon dried basil
1 teaspoon marjoram

½ teaspoon oregano
salt and pepper, to taste
2 medium courgettes,
  thinly sliced
5 medium tomatoes,
  skinned and cut into
  chunks
4 oz (½ cup or 120 ml)
  tomato juice or water
  (if needed)
1 tablespoon capers
  (optional)

1. Heat olive oil in a pot. Add onion and garlic; sauté until onion is transparent, about 5 minutes.
2. Add aubergine (eggplant), peppers, wine, and seasonings. Mix well. Cover and simmer until vegetables are tender, about 15 minutes.
3. Add courgettes and tomatoes. Continue to simmer, covered, a further 30 minutes or longer, until all vegetables are very tender. (Add tomato juice or water as needed.)
4. Add capers, if you want to, during the last 15 minutes of cooking.
5. Chill to serve as an appetizer.

Serves 6

Courgettes à la Grecque

Here is another recipe that is equally good eaten hot (as a vegetable accompaniment to a main course) or cold—a first course served as a salad on lettuce leaves.

5-6 tablespoons olive oil
2 large onions, thinly sliced
2 large cloves of garlic, crushed
8 small-medium courgettes, sliced into rounds
6 medium tomatoes, skinned, seeded, and chopped
1 tablespoon lemon juice
1 tablespoon fresh chopped tarragon (or 1 teaspoon dried)
pinch of thyme
salt
freshly ground black pepper

1. Heat the oil in a frying pan. Sauté the onions until they are soft and transparent.
2. Add the minced garlic to the pan together with the sliced courgettes (about ½ inch or 1 cm thick) and cook for a few minutes.
3. Add the tomatoes and lemon juice.
4. Mix in tarragon, thyme and salt and pepper to taste.
5. Simmer gently for about 45 minutes.

Serves 8

Courgette Fritters

This makes a delicious warm appetizer snack but can also go well as a hot side dish with grilled meat.

1/8 oz (2-3 g) fresh yeast or ½ teaspoon dried
pinch of salt
1 teaspoon warm water
2 teaspoons olive oil
2 oz (60 g) or 6 level tablespoons plain flour
1 egg white
2 small-medium courgettes, thinly sliced
oil for deep frying

1. First make the batter by placing yeast, salt and warm water into a preheated mixing bowl. When the yeast and salt are dissolved, add the oil and flour. Work the mixture together with your fingers. Cover and allow to stand for two hours in a warm place.
2. Slice courgettes thinly.
3. Heat oil in a deep fryer to 375°F (190°C).
4. Beat the egg white until stiff and fold into the batter mixture when it is ready. Coat the courgette slices in batter and fry in the hot oil until golden brown. Remove and drain on paper towels. Serve right away.

Serves 4

Zucchini Fritters

This version of a fritter appetizer is made without yeast.

1 lb (450 g) zucchini
flour
salt and freshly ground black pepper
oil for deep-frying
2 egg whites

1. Cut courgettes into strips. Sprinkle with salt and allow to stand for 30 minutes. Rinse, drain, and dry on paper towels.
2. Heat oil until a crumb put into it sizzles actively.
3. Toss zucchini in flour seasoned with salt and pepper. Then coat them in the egg whites which have been whisked until stiff but not quite dry.
4. Fry until they are brown. Drain on paper towels, season with salt and pepper, and serve immediately.

Serves 4

Zucchini and Mushrooms in Soy Sauce

Here is another recipe that can also be used as a cold first course or a hot main course accompaniment and will go a long way toward decreasing a zucchini crop bonanza.

10 small courgettes
2 oz (50 g) butter
8 oz (225 g) mushrooms, sliced
2 tablespoons soy sauce
10 fl oz (300 ml) light cream
salt and freshly ground black pepper

1. Cut the courgettes into 1-inch (2.5 cm) slices.
2. Melt the butter in a shallow pan. Add courgettes to the melted butter and cook over low heat for about 15 minutes, stirring occasionally.
3. Add sliced mushrooms, soy sauce, cream, and salt and pepper.
4. Raise the heat and cook with the cream boiling for 5 minutes.
5. Cool and serve as a cold appetizer. Or transfer to a heated dish and serve as a side vegetable.

Serves 8

Zucchini Parmesan

*Hard and pungent Parmesan cheese can be grated in the food
processor. Simply cut the cheese into cubes before processing.
Served at room temperature, these zucchini strips are a fine
appetizer.*

4 small zucchini
2 oz (¼ cup or 50 g) bread crumbs
3 oz (1/3 cup or 75 g) freshly grated Parmesan cheese
½ teaspoon dried rosemary
1/8 teaspoon red or cayenne pepper
½ teaspoon salt
¼ teaspoon freshly ground pepper
1 egg
oil

1. Cut each zucchini in half lengthwise and cut in half lengthwise
   again. Cut the strips in half widthwise.
2. In a shallow dish, combine bread crumbs, Parmesan cheese,
   rosemary, and spices. Blend well.
3. In another shallow dish, beat the egg lightly. Dip each zucchini
   piece first in the egg and then in the cheese mixture, coating
   evenly.
4. Place them in a single layer on a lightly-oiled baking tray.
   Bake in a preheated oven at 400°F (200°C) for 5 to 7 minutes.
   Turn over and bake a further 5 minutes or until crisp and lightly
   browned.
5. Remove from oven and serve.

4 servings

Marinated Courgettes and Aubergines

A pleasant first course to prepare in advance.

3 small-medium (about 1 lb or 450 g) courgettes
1 lb (450 g) aubergines (eggplant)
salt and freshly ground pepper
olive oil
8 oz (240 ml) white wine vinegar
4 tablespoons white wine
juice of 1 lemon
1 carrot, diced
1 large onion, chopped
5 sage leaves, cut into small pieces
3 juniper berries
2 sprigs parsley, chopped
1 bay leaf

1. Cut courgettes and aubergines into quarters lengthways.
2. Sprinkle with salt, place in a colander, and allow to stand for 30 minutes.
3. Rinse and dry them and fry in olive oil until lightly browned. As they become tender, remove them to a baking dish, skin side up. (The aubergines need more time than the courgettes to cook.)
4. Combine remaining ingredients in a large saucepan. Bring to a boil, then lower heat and simmer for 2 minutes.
5. Pour the hot vinegar marinade over the cooked vegetables. Cover and refrigerate for 2 days.
6. Remove bay leaf and serve at room temperature.

8 servings

49

Courgette Timbales

A timbale is a custard-like dish (of vegetables in this case) baked in a drum-shaped mold or ramekin.

1 lb (450 g) courgettes, grated
salt
2 eggs plus 1 egg yolk
2 oz (50 g) fresh fine white breadcrumbs
10 fl oz (300 ml) milk
1 tablespoon fresh thyme, chopped
freshly ground pepper
salt to taste

1. Grate courgettes and sprinkle with salt. Allow to stand in a colander for half an hour. Rinse and dry well on paper towels.
2. Grease well (with oil) 6 ramekin dishes and set aside.
3. Beat together the eggs and egg yolk. Add the grated courgettes and the rest of the ingredients and mix well.
4. Spoon the mixture into the prepared ramekin dishes. Cover with lightly oiled greaseproof paper. Place in a large pan of water (or a bain-marie) in an oven preheated to 325°F (170°C) and bake until the timbales are set, about 40 minutes. Serve warm.

Serves 6

Mediterranean Vegetables with Tahini

This is an easy starter because it can be prepared in advance. Tahini, a paste made from sesame seeds, combines with the grilled vegetables to create a festive first course.

2 peppers, seeded and cut into quarters
2 courgettes, cut in half lengthways
2 small aubergines, cut in half lengthways
1 fennel bulb, cut into quarters
olive oil
salt and pepper to taste

Tahini sauce:
8 oz (1 cup or 225 g) tahini paste
2 cloves garlic, minced
2 tablespoons olive oil
2 tablespoons lemon juice
4 fl oz (½ cup or 120 ml) cold water

1. Brush vegetables with oil. Grill or barbecue just until they brown, turning them over once. (Peel off the skin if the peppers blacken.)
2. Season with salt and freshly ground black pepper and leave them to cool.
3. Make tahini sauce by mixing all ingredients except water in a food processor. Then, add water while motor is running, continuing to process until the mixture is smooth.
4. Arrange vegetables on a platter and dribble sauce over it. Serve at room temperature with pitta bread.

Serves 4

Hummus with Courgettes

This Middle Eastern rendition adds to the enormous variety of ways to serve courgettes. It can also use fried aubergine (eggplant) slices.

1 can chick peas
2 cloves garlic
6 tablespoons lemon juice
4 tablespoons tahini paste
5 tablespoons olive oil
1 teaspoon ground cumin
salt and freshly ground black pepper, to taste
1 lb (450 g) small courgettes, unpeeled
paprika

1. Drain the chick peas, setting the liquid aside, and blend them in a food processor together with the garlic until you have a smooth paste. Add some liquid from the tin if necessary.
2. Add the lemon juice and tahini and continue to process until smooth. Then, while still processing, add 3 tablespoons of the olive oil.
3. Add the cumin and salt and pepper. Mix. Transfer the smooth mixture into a covered bowl until ready to use.
4. Cut the unpeeled small courgettes lengthways into halves. In a large frying pan, heat the remaining oil and fry the courgettes, sprinkled with salt and pepper, until just tender, about 2-3 minutes on each side.
5. Arrange the courgettes on four plates and heap a portion of hummus, garnished with paprika, on each plate. Serve with pitta bread.

Serves 4

Zucchini Bruschetta

*The medley of herbs enlivens the zucchini and produces this
excellent and zesty treat to whet the appetite.*

4-6 small zucchini (about 1 ½ lbs or 700 g)
4 tablespoons olive oil
2 cloves garlic, crushed
1 tablespoon shredded fresh basil
1 tablespoon chopped fresh parsley
½ teaspoon oregano
salt and pepper
**8 crostini (thin and lightly toasted slices of French or
    Italian bread)**
about 3 oz (80 g) Swiss or other hard cheese, thinly sliced

1. Cut zucchini into strips about the size of french fries or chips.
2. Add zucchini to oil that has been heated in a large frying pan
    and cook over medium heat for about 10 minutes, stirring
    occasionally. When lightly browned, add garlic, basil, parsley,
    and oregano. Sprinkle in some salt and a few grinds of pepper.
    Cook for 2 more minutes, stirring frequently. Remove from
    heat.
3. Spoon the zucchini mixture onto bread slices that have been
    arranged on a baking sheet. Cover with a slice of cheese and
    bake in preheated oven at 400°F (200°C), just until the cheese
    melts, about 4-5 minutes. Serve right away.

Serves 4

Fried Stuffed Zucchini Flowers

*The zucchini plant produces female flowers, from which the
fruit grows, and non-fruit-bearing male flowers. The flower is
edible and delicious when fried or used in other dishes.*

3 oz (½ cup or 80 g) flour
1 tablespoon olive oil
12 tightly closed zucchini flowers, washed and dried
1 oz (¼ cup or 25 g) coarse bread crumbs
6 anchovy fillets, mashed
1 tablespoon chopped parsley
oil for deep frying
salt and pepper to taste

1. Mix together the flour and oil and add just enough water to
   produce a batter that is not too liquid.
2. Remove the central piece or pistil from the zucchini flowers.
3. Soak bread crumbs in milk and squeeze them dry. Mix them
   together with the anchovies and parsley. Stuff the flowers with
   the mixture, pressing to close the flower around the filling.
4. Preheat oil to 350°F (180°C). Coat stuffed flowers with batter
   and deep fry them until golden all over.
5. Season with salt and pepper, drain on paper towels, and serve
   immediately.

Serves 4

Italian Zucchini Flowers

Italians stuff the exquisite zucchini flowers with mozzarella,
coat them in a light batter, and fry them in hot olive oil.

12 fresh zucchini flowers
2 eggs
¼ teaspoon salt
8 fl oz (1 cup or 240 ml) water
8 oz (1¼ cups or 200 g) flour
mozzarella

1. Choose a fresh bunch of a dozen flowers. Carefully remove hard central piece. Do not wash. Pat dry any moisture.
2. To make the batter, beat eggs with salt and pour in water and flour. Mix well to a smooth consistency.
3. Place a thin strip of mozzarella cheese inside each flower, and dip in the batter.
4. Fry in oil that is hot but not smoking until golden and crispy. Drain on paper towels and serve immediately.

Serves 4 or 6

Baked Stuffed Zucchini Flowers

If you're intrigued with zucchini flowers, here's one version of the delicate flower that makes a gorgeous luxury and insures good dinner conversation.

12 courgette flowers
1 ½ oz (40 g) pine nuts
1 ½ (40 g) breadcrumbs
6 mushrooms, finely chopped
a few tarragon leaves, chopped (optional)
1-2 tablespoons white wine
salt and pepper
2-3 tablespoons walnut or hazelnut oil

1. Open up the flower and carefully take out the hard central piece, the pistil.
2. Mix pine nuts, breadcrumbs, and mushrooms. Add tarragon if you want to. Moisten the mixture with a little white wine.
3. Use your fingers to gently fill the flowers with the stuffing mixture.
4. Lay them in a baking dish. Sprinkle with salt and pepper and brush with some of the oil.
5. Bake in a moderate oven at 350°F (180°C) for about 12 minutes. Pour remaining oil over the baked flowers and serve.

Serves 6

Lunch or Supper

Pisto

*You may scramble lightly beaten eggs into it, stirring as if making scrambled eggs, to change its designation from Spanish to French as it yields a **pipérade**.*

4 tablespoons olive oil
1 medium onion, finely chopped
2 cloves garlic, crushed
2 tablespoons fresh chopped parsley (or 1 teaspoon dry)
4 red or green peppers, sliced and seeded
1 lb (450 g) small zucchini, peeled and chopped
1 lb (450 g) tomatoes
½ lb (225 g) new potatoes, cooked
salt and pepper

1. Heat the oil in a pan and add the onion, garlic, and parsley. Cover and cook gently until onions are limp.
2. Add the peppers and continue to cook in a covered pan for another 10 minutes.
3. Add the chopped zucchini and tomatoes and continue cooking slowly, covered, for another 20 minutes.
4. Mix in the cubed potatoes, which have been separately fried to a golden color in olive oil until golden and tender but not too soft. Cook for a further 10 minutes.
5. Season with salt and pepper and serve.

Serves 4

Courgette Omelet

Other vegetables can be used in place of, or in addition to, the ones mentioned.

4 eggs
1 tablespoon butter or 1 oz (25 g) olive oil or half and
  half
1 or 2 small courgettes
quarter of a fresh green pepper
3 medium mushrooms
1-2 spring onions, chopped
salt and pepper to taste

1. Whisk the eggs for a few seconds. Add a dash of water (about ½ oz or 12 g) and stir. Set aside.
2. Slice peeled courgettes thinly and also cut green pepper, mushrooms, and spring onions into thin slices.
3. Melt butter and/or olive oil in a 10-inch (25 cm) omelet pan (if unavailable, use a non-stick frying pan). When butter starts to sizzle, add the slices of courgettes, mushrooms, and green peppers. Turn down the heat slightly. Stir the vegetables. Just when they start to turn brown, add a bit more olive oil if necessary, and pour in the egg mixture. Add the pieces of spring onion and sprinkle spices liberally over the entire mixture.
4. As the omelet starts to form, carefully lift one edge of the omelet and tilt the pan so that the uncooked egg runs under the cooked portion. Do this in as many places as necessary until all of the egg has formed. Fold the omelet in half. Reduce heat and carefully turn the folded omelet over so that the upper side is now in contact with the pan. Let it cook for another 30 seconds and then divide in half and serve hot.

Serves 2

Zucchini Pancake

An easy vegetable treat to go well with salad or a simple course such as grilled chicken.

2 medium zucchini, grated and squeezed dry
1 small potato, peeled and grated
1 small onion, grated
1 clove garlic, minced
2 tablespoons flour
2 eggs, slightly beaten
salt and pepper
2 teaspoons butter (sunflower oil may be substituted)
1 tablespoon fresh Parmesan cheese (optional)

1. Grate zucchini, potato, onion, and garlic in a food processor and combine them in a bowl together with the flour, eggs, and salt and pepper to taste.
2. Melt 1 teaspoon of the butter in a 10-inch (25 cm) non-stick frying pan over moderate heat.
3. Put the zucchini mixture in the pan, shaping it with a spatula. Cook, uncovered, over medium heat until the edges are golden and the bottom is firm and crisp (10-12 minutes). Turn over by placing a large plate over the pan and inverting the pancake onto it.
4. Melt the remaining butter in the pan, and slide the pancake back into the pan. Cook until firm (about 8-10 minutes).
5. Sprinkle with Parmesan cheese, if you want to, and serve.

Serves 4

Zucchini-Carrot Kugel

*This recipe will add further proof—if further proof is needed—
that zucchini is not a tedious or uninteresting vegetable.*

3-4 medium zucchini, coarsely grated
3 medium onions, finely chopped
3 tablespoons butter
5 medium carrots, coarsely grated
3 large eggs, beaten
**3 ½-4 oz (¾ cup or 110 g) matzo meal or fine
   breadcrumbs**
6 tablespoons flour
1 teaspoon baking powder
freshly ground black pepper
2 tablespoons butter for dotting the top

1. Salt zucchini and allow to stand in a colander for 30 to 40 minutes. Squeeze out remaining water.
2. In a heavy pan sauté the onion in butter over medium heat until limp and transparent (about 5 minutes). Remove from heat.
3. Turn sautéed onions into a large bowl and mix together with the grated zucchini and grated carrots.
4. Add the beaten eggs and the matzo meal (or breadcrumbs).
5. Sift in the flour and baking powder, and grind in black pepper. Mix well.
6. Turn the batter into a well-greased 9x13 inch (23x31 cm) baking pan. Scatter small bits of butter on the top.
7. Bake in oven preheated to 375°F (190°C) for 1¼ hours.

Serves 4-6

Zucchini-Carrot Latkes

These pancakes, which will enliven any repast, can be made in advance. When ready to serve, place them on a baking sheet and heat them in a 400°F (200°C) oven.

4 large zucchini, shredded
4 large carrots, shredded
2-3 spring onions, chopped
4 eggs, beaten
4 oz (½ cup or 110 g) flour
2 teaspoons baking powder
½ teaspoon nutmeg
pinch of cardamom
salt and pepper, to taste
oil for frying, preferably peanut oil

1. Shred the carrots and zucchini in a food processor and place in a large bowl. Add the spring onions and beaten eggs. Blend it all together.
2. Add the flour, baking powder, nutmeg, cardamom, salt and pepper. Mix well.
3. Heat oil in a large frying pan. Drop the mixture by spoonfuls into the oil. When pancakes are set, turn them over, and continue to fry until they are crisp. Remove them and place on absorbent paper towels to remove any excess oil and serve.

Serves 6

Frittata of Courgettes

Serve this quick supper or lunch with a green salad and crusty bread.

1 tablespoon olive oil
4 medium courgettes, thinly sliced
1 red pepper, cut into thin slices
1-2 cloves garlic, chopped
6 eggs, lightly beaten
4 tablespoons sun-dried tomatoes,
  drained of oil and chopped
2-3 spring onions, chopped
2 tablespoons fresh basil or mint or a mixture of both
salt and pepper
1 oz (25 g) grated cheese such as cheddar

1. Heat oil in a large frying pan and cook the courgettes, red pepper, and garlic for about 10 minutes, until soft. Stir occasionally.
2. Whisk the eggs in a bowl and add tomatoes, spring onions, herbs and seasonings. Mix it all together.
3. Reduce heat under the pan and pour in the egg mixture, allowing it to run under the vegetables. Cook over a low heat until the base is golden.
4. Sprinkle cheese over the top and place the pan under preheated hot grill until the cheese melts. Cut into wedges.

Serves 6-8

Courgette Soufflé

Souffles are not necessarily tricky or difficult, and this one could become a great favorite. It can be prepared in advance up to step 3. Then, when ready to serve, reheat gently before folding in the whipped egg whites.

2 tablespoons
  breadcrumbs
2 small courgettes
  (about 14 oz or 400 g)
4 tablespoons butter
1 onion, finely chopped
3 tablespoons flour
6 fl oz (¾ cup or 180 ml)
  milk
4 fl oz (½ cup or 120 ml)
  cream

salt and pepper
¼ teaspoon nutmeg
4 egg yolks
6 tablespoons
  cheddar
3 tablespoons
Parmesan cheese,
  grated
6 egg whites

1. Cook courgettes for just a few minutes, until tender; drain, chop and purée them in a blender or food processor.
2. Cook the onion in melted butter until soft. Add flour and cook another 2 minutes. Add milk, cream, and courgette purée. Stir in salt and pepper to taste and nutmeg.
3. Remove from heat and beat in the egg yolks together with the cheddar and Parmesan. (Stop here if you are preparing in advance.)
4. Beat the egg whites until stiff and fold into the mixture.
5. Pour the mixture into 8 ramekin dishes which have been buttered and sprinkled with breadcrumbs. Sprinkle a little extra Parmesan cheese over the ramekins.
6. Bake at 400°F oven (200°C) for 12-15 minutes.

Serves 8

Vegetable Quiche

Ingredients can be varied according to what you have available in your garden.

pastry
2 tablespoons olive oil
1 large onion, chopped
2 cloves garlic, minced
3 courgettes, sliced
4 carrots, sliced
4 oz (100 g) peas
1 lb ((450 g) mushrooms,
  sliced
1 tablespoon tamari (or
  Japanese soy sauce)

12 oz (350 g) cheddar
  or other hard
  cheese, grated
7 eggs
5 fl oz (150 ml) milk
salt and pepper, to
  taste
3 tablespoons light or
  single cream

1. Line a greased flan dish with pastry.
2. Heat the oil in a pan and sauté all vegetables except mushrooms. When onions have softened, add mushrooms and cook a few minutes longer.
3. Remove from heat. Add tamari and blend ingredients together.
4. Fill the pastry-lined flan dish with half the cheese, then vegetables, then the rest of the cheese.
5. In a large bowl, beat the egg together with the milk, and season with salt and pepper. Pour this mixture over all. Then slowly decant the cream into the middle of the quiche.
6. Bake at 275°F (140°C) for 50 minutes, until the color is golden and the center is firm.

Serves 6

65

Zucchini Pudding

This is a popular dairy dish of the Eastern Mediterranean that is also good served cold in the summertime.

4 zucchini (about 2 lbs or 1 kg)
3 eggs, beaten
½ lb (225 g) coarse farmer or cottage cheese
½ teaspoon salt
2 oz (¼ cup or 50 g) herbed breadcrumbs
butter

1. Peel the zucchini and grate coarsely.
2. Mix zucchini with beaten eggs, cheese, salt and breadcrumbs.
3. Turn the mixture into a well-buttered baking dish, 8 x 8 inches (20 x 20 cm).
4. Bake in a 350°F (180°C) oven for a half hour or until brown.
5. Cut into squares and serve warm.

Serves 4

Vegetable Kebabs

*Here's one that can be done on the outside barbecue with a
variety of fresh vegetables from the garden. Serve on a bed of
rice with garlic bread for a pleasant summer supper.*

2 zucchini, cut into 1-inch (3 cm) slices
2 yellow zucchini, cut into 1-inch (3 cm) slices
2 large green peppers, cut into 1-inch (3 cm) squares
2 large red sweet peppers, cut into 1-inch (3 cm) squares
1 medium onion, quartered
1 bottle Italian salad dressing

1. Place vegetables in a bowl and add Italian dressing. Mix well
    and marinate for an hour.
2. Remove vegetables from marinade, reserving marinade, and
    thread them alternately on skewers.
3. Place skewers of kebabs on the grate and cook for 10 to 15
    minutes, brushing with marinade during cooking and turning
    once halfway through.

Serves 4

Stuffed Pasta Shells

*Serve with a salad to make a satisfying, calorie-conscious
Italian repast.*

6 oz (175 g) jumbo shells, uncooked
15 oz (1 ¾ cups or 425 g) low-fat ricotta cheese
4 oz (1 cup or 100-125 g) shredded low-fat
   mozzarella cheese
3 tablespoons grated Parmesan cheese
1 unpeeled medium zucchini, finely shredded
   and well drained
1 carrot, finely-shredded
few sprigs of flat leaf parsley, chopped
1 clove garlic, minced
½ teaspoon oregano
salt and pepper, to taste
16 oz (450 g) tomato sauce

1. Cook pasta shells according to directions on package. Drain and place them separately on a plate or waxed paper to prevent them from sticking together.
2. Combine remaining ingredients, except sauce, in a bowl. Mix well.
3. Fill each pasta shell with about 1 ½ tablespoons of this mixture.
4. Cover the bottom of a 6 x 10 inch (15 x 25 cm) baking dish with a thin spread of some of the sauce. Arrange shells in the dish, cheese side up. Spoon remaining sauce over shells.
5. Cover and bake in 350°F (180°C) oven for 35 minutes.

6 servings

Courgette Boats

Shirley, who gave me this recipe, often prepares it ahead of time or freezes it for future use. For a complete meal, serve with a salad and wholelmeal bread and butter.

4 large courgettes (about ½ lb or 225 g each)
2 large onions, finely chopped
2 stalks of celery, chopped
2-3 garlic cloves, minced
2 tablespoons olive oil
l large tin of tomatoes
bunch of freshly chopped parsley
salt and pepper, to taste
2 oz (50 g) grated cheese

1. Steam the washed but unpeeled courgettes for five minutes.
2. Split them lengthwise. Scoop out the soft yellow centers, chop finely, and put aside. Place the courgette boats in a baking dish.
3. Fry the chopped onions and celery and the minced garlic in olive oil.
4. Add the chopped courgette pulp to the pan. Add the tin of chopped tomatoes (or fresh tomatoes) and the parsley.
5. Mix it all together and cook, stirring occasionally. Season as required.
6. Fill the courgette boats with the mixture. Sprinkle with the grated cheese and bake at 350°F (180° C) for about 30 minutes.

Serves 4

Zucchini Ripiene

Serve this Italian version of courgette boats with a crisp salad.

4 medium courgettes
1 medium onion
2 garlic cloves, minced
1 tablespoon olive oil
2 tomatoes
1 teaspoon finely chopped oregano leaves
salt and pepper to taste
Parmesan cheese
breadcrumbs

1. Wash the courgettes and split them lengthwise. Steam for five minutes, then scoop out the center pulp and chop this finely.
2. Place the boat-shaped zucchini cases in a baking dish.
3. Fry the finely-chopped onion and garlic in olive oil, together with the zucchini pulp, for 5 minutes. Add skinned, chopped, and deseeded tomatoes, oregano, and seasonings. Blend together and cook for a further 5 minutes.
4. Spoon the mixture into the zucchini cases, top with a layer of Parmesan cheese and sprinkle with fine breadcrumbs.
5. Bake for 15 minutes in preheated oven at 375°F (190° C).

Serves 4

Mediterranean Zucchini Bake

This vegetarian course combines ingredients and flavors to create an attractive and tasty dish.

4 medium zucchini, about 2 lbs (900 g)
4 eggs
½-1 teaspoon salt
¼ teaspoon freshly ground black pepper
8 oz (1½ cups or 225 g) fine bread crumbs
7 oz (1 cup or 200 g) freshly grated Parmesan cheese
a handful of fresh basil leaves, cut into small pieces
2 teaspoons chopped fresh thyme, or 1 teaspoon dried thyme
2 tablespoons chopped fresh flat-leaf parsley
olive oil
1 lb (450 g) mozzarella, cut into thin slices
2-3 medium tomatoes, thinly sliced

1. Cut zucchini lengthwise into very thin slices.
2. In a bowl, beat the eggs lightly. Add salt and pepper and set aside.
3. In another bowl mix together the bread crumbs, Parmesan cheese, basil, thyme, and parsley and set aside.
4. Oil the bottom of a 12 x 14-inch (30 x 36 cm) baking dish. Arrange a layer of zucchini slices on the bottom, followed by a layer of mozzarella, then a layer of tomato slices. Sprinkle over it some of the bread crumb mixture and drizzle lightly with olive oil. Repeat the layers until all the vegetables are used up, ending with a layer of mozzarella. Pour the egg mixture evenly over the top.

5. Bake in a preheated oven at 350° F (180°C) for about 45 minutes or until the eggs are set and the top is golden. If it starts browning too quickly, cover with aluminum foil and remove the foil for the last 5 minutes of baking.

6. Allow it to settle for 10 minutes after removing from the oven. Then cut into squares. May be served warm or cold.

Serves 6-8

Risotto with Spring Vegetables

Although risotto is easy to cook, you need to watch it. Stirring almost constantly while gradually adding wine, rice and vegetables yields a moist, yet slightly nutty result. Besides, how can it be bad with all that wine?

4 oz (125 g) butter, divided into quarters
2 medium onions, finely chopped
2 large cloves garlic, finely chopped
1 medium zucchini, cut into small pieces
4 oz (1 cup or 110 g) fresh green peas
2 carrots, diced
1 tomato, peeled and cut into small pieces
16 fl oz (2 cups or 450 ml) dry white wine
1 lb (450 g) Italian Arborio or short grain rice
48 fl oz (6 cups or 1.4 litres) boiling stock
2 oz (½ cup or 50 g) finely grated Italian cheese such as parmigiano or romano
salt and freshly ground pepper

1. Melt 1 quarter of the butter in a small saucepan on low heat and cook half the chopped onion and garlic in it together with all of the vegetables, stirring frequently.
2. When the onion is soft and golden, add half of the wine and simmer until wine has evaporated. Set aside.
3. Melt 2 more quarters of the butter in a large pot and add the remaining onion and garlic, cooking and stirring until the onion is soft. Add the rice, stirring until it is well mixed together. Then pour in the remaining wine and stir until the wine is absorbed.

73

4. Add one cup of boiling stock at a time, stirring until each cupful is absorbed before adding more, until it is used up. Rice should be creamy but slightly nutty in texture and completely cooked in about 20 minutes.

5. Stir in the vegetable mixture which has been set aside. Add the remaining butter and half the cheese. Add salt and freshly ground pepper to taste.

6. Serve right away with remaining cheese served separately.

Serves 6

Spicy African Stew

The unusual blend of ingredients and flavors makes a satisfying party delight.

1 tablespoon oil
1 medium onion, chopped
1 medium sweet potato, peeled and diced
2 garlic cloves, crushed
32 fl oz (4 cups or 1 litre) chicken stock
5 ½-6 oz (¾ cup or 175 g) uncooked white rice
1 teaspoon thyme
½ teaspoon cumin
½-1 teaspoon salt
16 fl oz (2 cups or 450 ml) tomato sauce
2 16-oz (450 g) tins chickpeas, drained and rinsed
1 medium zucchini, sliced
6 oz (175 g) peanut butter

1. Heat the oil in a large pot. Sauté onion, sweet potato and garlic until the onion is tender.
2. Stir in the stock, rice, thyme, cumin, and salt and bring to a boil. Then reduce heat.
3. Simmer for 20 minutes, stirring frequently, until the rice and vegetables are tender.
4. Mix in the tomato sauce, chickpeas and zucchini. Simmer for 15 minutes, stirring occasionally, until zucchini is tender.
5. Stir in the peanut butter.
6. Ladle into soup bowls and serve with crusty French bread.

8 servings

Pitta with Courgettes and Carrots

Most of the preparation can be done in advance, but do not fill the pitta breads too soon or the salad mixture will make the pitta bread soggy.

2 carrots
1 oz (25 g) pecan nuts (or walnuts)
4 spring onions, sliced
2 fl oz (¼ cup or 50 ml) Greek yogurt
8 teaspoons olive oil
1 teaspoon lemon juice
1 tablespoon chopped fresh mint
2 courgettes
flour
salt and freshly ground black pepper
2 pitta breads
shredded lettuce

1. Place coarsely-grated carrots in a bowl. Add pecans and spring onions and mix well.
2. In another bowl, whisk the yogurt with 2 teaspoons of the olive oil, lemon juice, and fresh mint. Turn this dressing into the carrot mixture and toss well. Chill in a covered bowl until needed.
3. Slice the unpeeled courgettes diagonally. Season flour with salt and pepper and dip the courgette slices in it.
4. Heat the rest of the oil in a large frying pan. Add the coated courgette slices and fry for 3-4 minutes, turning once, until browned. Drain on paper towels.
5. Fill the slit or pocket of each pitta bread with the carrot mixture and courgette slices. Serve on shredded lettuce.

Serves 2

Pizza with Courgettes

*There are few hard and fast rules for topping ingredients,
which come in infinite varieties; this recipe could be called
pizza-with-anything or pizza-as-you-like-it.*

basic pizza shell
tomato sauce
garlic, sliced or chopped
oregano and basil
other spices—thyme, bay leaf, fennel, parsley
salt and pepper
mozzarella cheese
2 small courgettes, sliced
other toppings—mushrooms, green pepper, onions,
  spinach, anchovies, etcetera
2 tablespoons grated Parmesan cheese
1 tablespoon olive oil

1. Parbake the crust for about 4 minutes to give the dough a spring and prevent the weight of ingredients from pressing on the dough and making it heavy.
2. Spread tomato sauce evenly over pizza base leaving only a small border. You can make your own sauce by cooking the following ingredients over low heat for about 10 minutes: 2 lbs (1 kg) ripe tomatoes; 2 tablespoons olive oil; 1 teaspoon sugar; salt. Discard watery liquid.
3. Spread garlic over the sauce and add oregano and basil.
4. Sprinkle other spices over all, selecting the ones you like in the quantities you like.
5. Place mozzarella, thinly sliced, over sauce.

6. Arrange thinly-sliced courgettes over all. Add sliced mushrooms, green pepper, onions—or whatever you select. (Add sausage or pepperoni, if you want to.)
7. Sprinkle Parmesan cheese over all.
8. Dribble olive oil over the pizza.
9. Bake in a hot oven (425°F or 220°C) for about twenty minutes or until crust is lightly browned and ingredients are cooked through.

Ciabatta Rolls with Courgettes and Tomato-Saffron Sauce

A creamy tomato sauce provides the basis for a yummy courgette "sandwich."

1 ½ lbs (700 g) small courgettes
1 tablespoon olive oil
2 shallots, chopped
small can chopped tomatoes
pinch of sugar (optional)
a few saffron threads
2 fl oz (50 ml or ¼ cup) light cream
salt and pepper
4 ciabatta rolls

1. Cut small unpeeled courgettes in half, then cut each half lengthways into quarters to make strips about 1½ inches (4 cm) long.
2. In a large frying pan, heat the oil; add the chopped shallots and sauté over medium heat for a minute or two.
3. Put the courgette strips into the pan and cook for 5-6 minutes, stirring frequently.
4. Stir in the tomatoes and sugar (if desired). Immerse saffron threads in a drop of hot water for a few minutes and add to the courgettes with the cream. Cook for 4 minutes, stirring occasionally. Season to taste.
5. Cut open the rolls which have been warmed, and fill them with the courgette and sauce mixture.

Serves 4

Casseroles

Zucchini Casserole

For a relaxing dinner party, prepare this the night before and leave it in the refrigerator to await the arrival of your guests before placing it in the oven.

2 tablespoons butter
2 medium onions, sliced
4-5 small zucchini
1 tin (1 lb or 450 g) tomatoes
salt to taste
grated cheese

1. Sauté the sliced onions in melted butter until golden.
2. Place onions in a casserole mixed together with sliced zucchini. Add tomatoes (fresh cut-up tomatoes may be substituted) and salt.
3. Cover and refrigerate.
4. When ready to cook, sprinkle grated cheese over top of casserole to cover all ingredients. Bake uncovered in 350° oven for 30-35 minutes.

Serves 6

Marrow Casserole

This is an excellent way to use zucchini that have become enormous after you've been away on holiday or forgotten to pick them. Overgrown zucchini—or marrows—have a high water content and do not lend themselves to steaming, but they are good baked in a casserole.

1 marrow (approximately 2 pounds or nearly 1 kg)
1 or 2 tomatoes
1 ½ ounces (40 g) butter
2 tablespoons mixed fresh herbs—tarragon, basil,
**   parsley, and chives**
salt and pepper

1. Peel the marrow and cut into 1-inch (2.5 cm) thick slices; cut into rough chunks, discarding the seeds.
2. Add quartered tomatoes and mix with fresh, chopped herbs. Season with salt and freshly ground pepper.
3. Butter an ovenproof dish and add the marrow with the remaining butter cut into small pieces.
4. Cover the dish and bake in pre-heated oven at 350°F (180°C) until just tender, about twenty minutes. Serve from the dish.

Serves 4 to 6

Zucchini Cheese Casserole

Made with low-fat cottage cheese, this is another low-calorie, low-cholesterol recipe to add to your heart healthy repertory.

3 medium zucchini, sliced
1 medium onion, chopped
2 tomatoes, sliced
2 tablespoons oil
1 lb (450 g) low-fat cottage cheese
1 teaspoon basil
½ teaspoon oregano
salt
3 oz (75 g) grated Parmesan cheese

1. Sauté zucchini slices and chopped onion in oil until golden.
2. Blend the cottage cheese well with basil and oregano and salt.
3. Alternate layers of zucchini, cottage cheese mixture, and tomato in casserole, and top with parmesan cheese.
4. Bake at 350°F (180°C) for 25-30 minutes. Uncover during last 10 minutes.

Serves 6

Zucchini Parmesan Casserole

Another easy version of zucchini with Parmesan cheese.

2 medium zucchinis (about 1 lb or 450 g)
1 tablespoon butter
1 teaspoon salt
1 teaspoon chopped parsley
4 tablespoons grated Parmesan cheese

1. Cut zucchini into thin slices and arrange them in a layer in a greased shallow baking dish.
2. Dot with some of the butter, and sprinkle with some of the salt, parsley and cheese.
3. Repeat layers until all ingredients are used, ending with cheese.
4. Bake in preheated oven at 400°F (200°C) for about 25 minutes, until zucchini is tender. If desired, place it under the grill just until the top is golden brown.

Serves 2-3

California Zucchini Cheese Casserole

Why California? Perhaps because Italians emigrated to that state and brought their familiar ingredients with them.

4 medium-large
  zucchini, sliced
l large can tomatoes,
  about 1 lb 12 oz (800 g
  or 3 ½ cups)
1 large green pepper,
  chopped
8 oz (225 g) mushrooms,
  sliced
¼ teaspoon basil
1 onion, chopped
¼ teaspoon oregano

½ teaspoon sugar
  (optional)
salt and pepper
12 oz (350 g) herb
  seasoned stuffing
  crumbs
4-6 oz (125-175 g)
  mozzarella cheese,
  shredded
2 oz (50 g) Parmesan
  cheese, grated

1. Parboil the zucchini and drain.
2. In a large bowl, combine all ingredients, except cheeses. Mix together and transfer to a casserole.
3. Sprinkle cheeses over the top and bake at 350°F (180°C) for 30 minutes.

Serves 8

86

Spicy Zucchini and Potato Mash

This spicy side dish goes well on any North African or Middle Eastern menu.

2 medium zucchini
2 potatoes
¾ teaspoon ground cumin
¼ teaspoon chili powder
½ teaspoon caraway seed
¼ teaspoon salt
1 tablespoon lemon juice
4 garlic cloves, crushed
2 tablespoons olive oil

1. Peel the zucchini, cut them into chunks, and cook in water until they are soft (about 20 minutes). Drain and mash coarsely.
2. Cook the potatoes in water until soft. Drain and mash coarsely. Mix them both together.
3. Mix the cumin, chili (use less if you prefer a less spicy taste), caraway, salt, lemon juice, and garlic together into a paste and stir it into the vegetables.
4. Put the mixture into a lightly buttered casserole. Dribble the olive oil over the top. When ready to serve, place the casserole in a 350°F (180°C) oven to heat through.

Serves 4-6

Zucchini Custard Casserole

Accompanied by a salad, this casserole makes a rich and simple one-dish supper that is also satisfying and colorful.

1 lb (450 g) zucchini, sliced
1 tablespoon minced onion
2 tablespoons olive or sunflower oil
3 eggs
4 fl oz (½ cup or 120 ml) milk
8-10 oz (225-280 g) cheddar cheese, grated
2 tablespoons dry bread crumbs
½ teaspoon salt
dash cayenne pepper
thyme, to taste

1. In a frying pan, sauté unpeeled zucchini and onion in oil until tender. Set aside.
2. In a large bowl, beat eggs and milk. Add one third of the cheese and the bread crumbs, salt, pepper, and thyme to milk-egg mixture. Stir in zucchini and onion.
3. Turn mixture into a greased casserole and sprinkle the top with the rest of the grated cheese.
4. Bake uncovered in 350°F (180°C) oven for 35-40 minutes.

Serves 3-4

Summer Zucchini and Mushroom Bake

Yellow (or green) zucchini may be substituted for the squash, especially if available in your overflowing vegetable garden.

1 small zucchini, cut into small cubes
1 small yellow squash, cut into small cubes
5-10 mushrooms, sliced
1 small (or ½ medium) red onion, thinly sliced
3-4 oz (80-100 g) mozzarella cheese, shredded
2 tablespoons shredded fresh basil or 1 tablespoon dried basil
salt

1. Combine zucchini, squash, mushrooms and red onion in a casserole and mix well. Sprinkle with the cheese and basil and salt.
2. Cover and bake at 350°F (180°C) for 25 to 30 minutes or until the vegetables are crisp.

Serves 4

Winter Stew

Perfect for cheering up an otherwise cheerless, cold-weather day.

1½-2 lbs (700-900 g) minced beef
1 small head of cabbage
1 small onion, chopped
2 stalks celery, chopped
1 large carrot, sliced
1 medium-large zucchini
1 small turnip, sliced
salt and freshly ground black pepper to taste
34 fl oz (about 4¼ cups or 1 litre) V-8 or tomato juice
8 oz (1 cup or 225 g) rice, bulgar, or barley

1. Brown the beef, drain off the fat, and put the beef in a casserole.
2. Place over it the cabbage, which has been cored and cut into small wedges, and the other vegetables. Season with salt and freshly ground black pepper.
3. Pour tomato juice over all and bake in oven at 325°F (170°C) for an hour.
4. Add the grain of your choice and more juice or water if necessary. Cook for another half hour, until grain is done.

Serves 6-8

Courgette Orange Bake

Goes well with beef or lamb dishes.

3-4 medium courgettes
4 large tomatoes, sliced
1 medium onion, chopped
1 tablespoon olive oil
1 tablespoon white wine vinegar
1 teaspoon sugar (optional)
½ teaspoon rosemary
grated rind and juice of half an orange
salt and pepper, to taste

1. Arrange overlapping slices of tomatoes and courgettes in a casserole.
2. Combine remaining ingredients and add to casserole.
3. Cover and bake in preheated oven at 350°F (180°C) for 20-25 minutes, until vegetables are tender.

Serves 4

Vegetable Macaroni Bake

Other pasta shapes may be used instead of macaroni.

8 oz (225 g) short cut
   macaroni
5 tablespoons butter
1 tablespoon flour
8 fl oz (1 cup or 250 ml)
   milk
4 oz (100 g) grated
   Parmesan cheese
½ teaspoon dry mustard
1 clove garlic, crushed
3 carrots, peeled and
   diced

1 red pepper
   (capsicum), seeded
   and sliced
2 zucchini, thinly sliced
4 oz (100 g) mushrooms,
   sliced
1 tablespoon tomato
   paste (purée)
½ teaspoon dried
   oregano
salt and pepper

1. Cook the macaroni in boiling water until barely tender, drain and rinse.

2. Melt 3 tablespoons butter in a pan, stir in the flour and cook for about a minute. Gradually add the milk and bring to the boil, stirring until thickened. Mix in just over half the cheese and the mustard.

3. In another pan, melt the remaining butter and add the garlic and carrots. Fry gently for a few minutes, then add the red pepper and cook for 2 minutes. Add the zucchini, mushrooms, tomato paste, oregano and salt and pepper. Cook for 3 to 4 minutes.

4. Put half the macaroni in a greased ovenproof dish and spoon the vegetable mixture over it. Add about a third of the sauce, then add the rest of the macaroni and the rest of the sauce.

5. Sprinkle the remaining cheese over the top and bake in a hot oven at 400°F (200°C) for 30 to 40 minutes, until bubbling and brown. Serve hot.

Serves 4-6

Zucchini-Spaghetti Casserole

Another easy way to use zucchini in a dish that can be given more color by leaving the zucchini unpeeled. It can also be prepared ahead of time, ready to go into the oven when your guests arrive.

4 oz (110 g) uncooked spaghetti, broken
1 large onion, chopped
1 green pepper, chopped
3 oz (80 g) butter
4 medium zucchini, sliced
4 medium tomatoes, cut in wedges
3-4 tablespoons fresh chopped parsley
salt and pepper to taste
6 oz (175 g) Swiss cheese, coarsely grated

1. Put broken spaghetti in a large pot of boiling water and boil gently until barely tender. Drain.
2. In a frying pan, cook onions and pepper in butter until tender, about 4 minutes. Add zucchini, cover and cook slowly for another 5-6 minutes. Stir in tomatoes, parsley, salt and pepper. Cover and cook until heated.
3. Put the mixture into a large casserole, and gently mix in the drained spaghetti. Spread cheese over the top. Bake in a 350°F (180°C) oven for 30 to 40 minutes.

Serves 4-5

Courgette and Potato Casserole

Although this recipe will serve six as an accompaniment, it could make a main meal to serve four.

1 tablespoon olive oil
12 oz (350 g) onions, chopped
14 oz (400 g) tin of chopped tomatoes
1 teaspoon tomato paste (purée)
½ teaspoon sugar
1 tablespoon chopped parsley
salt and freshly ground black pepper, to taste
6 tablespoons water
1 lb (450 g) potatoes, thinly sliced
2 medium-large courgettes (about 1 lb or 450 g), sliced

1. Heat half the oil in a frying pan, add the onions and cook gently over medium heat until soft and golden.
2. Add the tomatoes, tomato purée, sugar, parsley, seasonings and water. Simmer for 5 minutes.
3. Layer the potatoes and courgettes in a large casserole. Pour tomato sauce over it.
4. Cover and bake in preheated oven at 350°F (180°C) for 1½-1¾ hours or until potatoes are done.

Serves 6

Italian Vegetable Casserole

This combination of colorful fresh vegetables, which forms the basis of so much Italian cooking, yields a good texture and a rich and flavorful casserole.

2 medium zucchini, sliced
1 small (about 8 oz or 225 g) eggplant (aubergine)
3 large tomatoes, sliced
3 tablespoons olive oil
1 oz (25 g) butter
salt and pepper
2 cloves garlic, crushed
½ teaspoon marjoram
4 oz (110 g) mozzarella cheese, thinly sliced

1. Slice eggplant thinly. Sprinkle with salt and allow to stand in a colander for 30 minutes. Rinse well and pat dry.
2. Heat olive oil and butter in a large pan and fry aubergine slices until they are soft. Arrange them in an ovenproof casserole. Then fry the zucchini in the remaining oil until they are soft. Layer zucchini and tomatoes over the aubergines. Pour any remaining pan juices over all. Season with salt and pepper. Sprinkle with garlic and marjoram.
3. Place mozzarella over the top.
4. Cover and bake in preheated oven at 350°F (180°C) for 35-45 minutes, until vegetables are tender.

Serves 4-6

Courgette and Aubergine Crumble

Great for a bumper crop of courgettes.

3 tablespoons olive oil
2 medium red onions,
  sliced
2 cloves garlic, chopped
8 courgettes, sliced and
  cut into semi-circles
2 small aubergines
  (eggplants), cut into
  cubes
1 teaspoon rosemary
1 teaspoon dried dill
  weed (or a handful of
  fresh)
½ teaspoon allspice
salt and pepper

10 tomatoes, chopped
2 tablespoons tomato
  paste (purée)
10 fl oz (300 ml)
  tomato juice
10 fl oz (300 ml)
  chicken or vegetable
  stock
8 oz (225 g) butter
12 oz (350 g)
wholewheat flour
8 oz (225 g) ground
  walnuts
8 oz (225 g) chopped
  walnuts

1. Heat oil in large pot and sauté onion and garlic until onions are soft. Add courgettes and aubergines, herbs and spices, and continue to cook for a few minutes.
2. Add tomatoes and tomato paste. Pour in tomato juice and stock. Simmer about 15-20 minutes. When vegetables are tender, turn them into a greased casserole.
3. For the topping, rub softened butter into flour, then add ground and chopped walnuts. Spoon the mixture evenly over the top.
4. Bake at 325°F (160°C) for 40-45 minutes.

Serves 8-10

Baked Courgette Casserole

Other vegetables—sliced new potatoes, aubergines, peppers— can also be used for the layers of this vegetarian dish.

2 lbs (nearly 1 kg) courgettes, sliced
1 medium onion, thinly sliced
14 oz (400 g) tin tomatoes
6 tablespoons olive oil
6 tablespoons vegetable or chicken stock
1 teaspoon brown sugar
2 cloves garlic, crushed
2 tablespoons parsley, chopped
salt and pepper, to taste
2 tablespoons wholemeal breadcrumbs
8-12 black pitted olives

1. Place a layer of courgettes in the bottom of a greased casserole, followed by a layer of sliced onion, then tomatoes (use fresh ones if you want to). Continue in this way until you have used up all the vegetables.
2. In a small bowl, combine 4 tablespoons of the olive oil, the stock, sugar, garlic, parsley, and salt and pepper. (Increase the amounts, if necessary, if you have used additional vegetables.) Mix well and pour over the vegetables.
3. Scatter the breadcrumbs and the rest of the oil over the top.
4. Bake in a moderate oven at 350°F (180°C) for 1 hour.
5. Garnish with black olives and serve.

Serves 4-6

Mashed Zucchini Casserole

*Add leftover cooked diced chicken, if desired, to serve as a
main course.*

**2 lbs (900 g) zucchini or marrow, cooked, drained and
 mashed
1 medium carrot, grated
1 medium onion, chopped
1 small can cream of chicken soup
4 oz (110 g) butter
1 small package herbed breadcrumb stuffing mix**

1. Cut unpeeled zucchini into small pieces and cook in water just
    until soft enough to mash.
2. Mix mashed zucchini together with grated carrot, chopped
    onion, and soup.
3. Melt the butter and blend with the breadcrumb stuffing mix.
4. Grease a baking dish and pat three quarters of the stuffing
    mixture into the bottom, like a crust. Spoon the zucchini mixture
    over it. Sprinkle remaining crumbs over the top.
5. Bake at 350°F (180°C) for 40 minutes.

Serves 8-10

Zucchini Couscous

This simple zucchini dish is made with couscous, a grain that offers an excellent and tasty way to boost fibre intake.

1 medium zucchini, chopped
2 tablespoons chopped spring onions
2 tablespoons soy sauce
2 tablespoons white wine
1 clove garlic, crushed
4 oz (110 g) uncooked couscous
5 fl oz (150 ml) water
1½ teaspoons butter

1. Combine zucchini, spring onions, soy sauce, white wine, and garlic in a casserole and mix. Add couscous, water, and dots of butter and stir well.
2. Bake in 350°F (180°C) oven for 30 minutes. Add more water if needed.

Serves 4

Vegetable Bourguignonne

The vegetables absorb the wine and herbs to make a satisfying vegetarian dish.

2 tablespoons olive oil
3 courgettes, cut into thick slices
2 medium carrots, sliced
2 leeks, sliced
1 lb (450 g) new potatoes
12 oz (350 g) small whole onions or shallots
1 lb (450 g) small button mushrooms
1 parsnip, sliced
3 celery stalks, sliced
2 bay leaves
3 tablespoons wholewheat flour
14 fl oz (1 ¾ cups or 400 ml) red wine
2 tablespoons tomato paste (purée)
2 tablespoons lemon juice
1 tablespoon dried sage
salt to taste
12 oz (350 g) grated hard cheese such as cheddar

1. Sauté vegetables in oil together with bay leaves for 20 minutes.
2. Stir in flour and cook for a minute. Then blend in wine, tomato paste, lemon juice, sage, and salt.
3. Bake in a casserole at 300°F (150° C) for about 50 minutes, until vegetables are tender.
4. During last 10 minutes sprinkle with cheese.

Serves 6

Main Courses

Neapolitan Zucchini and Aubergine with Pasta

*My vegetarian friends appreciate this satisfying and
substantial dish.*

8 oz (225 g) pasta shells
2 medium onions, sliced
3 large cloves garlic,
　sliced
3 red peppers, cut into
　strips
4 tablespoons olive oil,
　plus a little more for
　the topping
2 aubergines (eggplants),
　diced
2 bay leaves

salt
1 teaspoon marjoram
1 teaspoon thyme
6 small zucchini,
　sliced
12 tomatoes, chopped
3 tablespoons tomato
　paste
6 oz (175 g) cheese,
　grated
14 oz (400 g) wholewheat
　breadcrumbs

1. Cook the pasta shells (or any other small shape such as
   bows).
2. Sauté onion, garlic and peppers in oil.
3. Add aubergines, bay leaves, salt and herbs.
4. Add zucchini, tomatoes and tomato paste and gently stir
   it all together.
5. Cover and simmer for about 20 minutes, until sauce
   thickens.
6. Mix in the cooked pasta shells, and put it all into an
   ovenproof casserole.
7. Make a gratin topping by combining cheese and
   breadcrumbs, moistened with a little oil, and spread the
   mixture over the top. Bake at 350°F (180°C) for 50
   minutes.

Serves 6

Lasagna with Zucchini

*Made with fresh herbs and vegetables, this lasagna variation
makes a wonderful summertime—or anytime—treat.*

4 tablespoons butter
4 tablespoons flour
16 fl oz (450 ml or 2 cups) milk
3 cloves garlic, crushed
1 tablespoon chopped thyme
salt and pepper
2 tablespoons olive oil
3 small-medium zucchini, sliced
tomatoes and mushrooms or eggplant (aubergine)
package of lasagna pasta
6-8 oz (175-225 g) Parmesan cheese, grated
buttered bread crumbs

1. Melt butter in a saucepan. Stir in flour, and cook but do not brown for 3 to 4 minutes. Remove from heat and whisk in milk all at once. Return to heat, stir and simmer until sauce thickens.
2. Add minced garlic, thyme, salt and pepper.
3. In a frying pan, heat olive oil and sauté sliced zucchini.
4. Place layer of lasagna pasta in large, lightly-oiled baking dish and cover with layer of sauce, layer of zucchini (and other selected vegetables), and sprinkling of cheese.
5. Repeat layers about six times and top the dish with buttered bread crumbs and more grated Parmesan cheese.
6. Bake uncovered at 350°F (180°C) for 30 minutes.

Serves 8

Zucchini Sausage Bake

*Couldn't be easier. Health- or cholesterol-conscious people can
use turkey or vegetarian sausages.*

1 lb (450 g) zucchini, chopped
1 clove garlic, sliced
1 medium onion, chopped
salt to taste
1 lb (450 g) sausage, cut up
3 eggs, beaten
6 oz (¾ cup or 175 g) Parmesan cheese, grated
15-20 oz (3-4 cups or 425-550 g) cooked rice

1. Mix all the ingredients together and spoon into a shallow baking dish.
2. Bake in a preheated oven at 300°F (150°C) for 1-1½ hours.

Serves 6

Courgette Tian

A tian is a typical Provencal-style gratin of vegetables. It can make a light main course served with rice or couscous or it can be a zestful side dish served with roast chicken or meat. Preparing it a day ahead can even improve the flavor.

4 tablespoon olive oil
2 medium onions, chopped
2 cloves garlic, chopped
salt and pepper to taste
1 tablespoon shredded fresh basil or oregano
3 medium courgettes, cut into ½ inch (1.2 cm) slices
3 medium tomatoes, thinly sliced
2 oz (½ cup or 50 g) grated Parmesan cheese

1. Heat 2 tablespoons of the oil in a frying pan over medium heat. Add onions and garlic and cook, stirring occasionally, until golden, about 10 minutes. Add salt and pepper.
2. Oil the bottom and sides of a 9 x 13 inch (23 x 31 cm) baking dish, and spread the mixture evenly into it. Sprinkle with half the herbs. Over the herbs, place alternating and slightly overlapping slices of zucchini and tomato. Sprinkle with remaining herbs and with the remaining 2 tablespoons of oil.
3. Bake the tian in a preheated oven at 375°F (190°C) until juices are sizzling, about 40-45 minutes. Sprinkle with cheese and bake for another 5 minutes. Remove from oven and allow it to rest for 10 minutes. Serve warm.

Serves 6

Rustic Vegetable Stew

This Mediterranean-style stew, which may be served over rice, calls only for crusty French bread as an accessory.

2 tablespoons olive oil
1 medium onion, chopped
3 garlic cloves, crushed
1 large potato, cut into ½-inch (1.2 cm) cubes
1 medium eggplant (aubergine), cut into 1-inch (2.5 cm) cubes
large tin (about 28 oz or 700 g) undrained tomatoes
12 fl oz water (1½ cups or 360 ml)
1 teaspoon salt
1 sprig fresh rosemary (or 1 teaspoon dried)
1 medium-large zucchini, sliced
1 green pepper, cut into 1-inch (2.5 cm) pieces
juice of 1 lemon
1 tablespoon chopped fresh dill (or 1 teaspoon dried)
freshly ground black pepper
feta cheese

1. Heat oil in a large pot and sauté the onions and garlic over medium heat until soft and golden. Add potato cubes and eggplant cubes. Mix in the juice from the tomatoes and the water. Add salt and rosemary and bring to a boil. Then reduce heat, and simmer covered for about 10 minutes.
2. Add sliced zucchini and pepper pieces. Continue to simmer, uncovered, for 5 minutes.
3. Add coarsely-chopped tomatoes together with lemon juice and dill, and simmer for another 5 minutes.
4. Add black pepper to taste and remove fresh rosemary sprig.
5. Top with crumbled feta cheese and serve.

Serves 4-6

Chili Sin Carne

This easy-to-prepare recipe for chili offers a beautiful blend of colors and flavors for a superb vegetarian course.

1 medium onion, chopped
½ green pepper, chopped
2 tablespoons olive oil
2-3 cloves garlic, crushed
1 large zucchini, chopped
1 carrot, diced
2 cans (15 oz or 425 g each) kidney beans
2 cans (about 1 lb or 450 g each) tomatoes, peeled and
  chopped
1-2 tablespoons chili powder
¼ teaspoon cumin
¼ teaspoon basil
¼ teaspoon oregano
¼ teaspoon thyme
freshly ground pepper to taste
4 fl oz (½ cup or 120 ml) water

1. In a large pot, sauté onion and green pepper in olive oil over medium heat until onions are soft, about 6-8 minutes.
2. Add garlic, zucchini and carrot and cook over low heat for a further 2 minutes.
3. Rinse and drain kidney beans and add them to the mixture together with tomatoes, seasonings, and water. Stir it all together.
4. Bring mixture to a boil, then reduce heat and simmer for about 35-45 minutes.

Serves 8

Gado-Gado

The richly flavored peanut sauce emanates from Indonesia. It is simple to make and goes well with many dishes. Here it is combined with lightly cooked vegetables to produce a popular Asian dish. As the selection and amount of vegetables may be varied depending on availability and imagination, or number of guests, it could become a popular dish in any kitchen.

2 large squares bean curd
oil for deep frying
zucchini, cut into strips
cauliflower florets
green beans
carrots, sliced diagonally
cabbage, shredded
3 hard-boiled eggs, quartered
boiled potatoes
cucumber, thinly sliced
lettuce, watercress or other salad greens

Peanut Sauce:
2-3 tablespoons peanut or sesame oil
4 shallots, finely chopped
2 cloves garlic, crushed
½ teaspoon chili powder
12 oz (350 g) chunky peanut butter
1 tablespoon lemon juice
1 tablespoon dark soy sauce
1 teaspoon brown sugar
salt to taste

1. Cut the bean curd into large slices and deep fry in hot oil until

golden brown. Remove and drain on absorbent paper.

2. Cut boiled eggs into quarters.

3. Prepare freshly cooked vegetables, by boiling separately for 3-4 minutes, so that they may be served warm or at room temperature.

4. Garnish a serving platter with salad greens around the edge. Arrange the bean curd and vegetables in the middle of the platter, placing the quartered eggs, sliced potatoes and cucumber on top. Spoon the peanut sauce over it.

5. For the peanut sauce, heat oil in a pan over low heat. Fry shallots and garlic until they become soft.

6. Add remaining ingredients to the pan, mixing thoroughly. Simmer on low heat for 10-15 minutes, stirring occasionally. Adjust amount of peanut butter if necessary to give a thick pouring consistency. Adjust seasonings.

Fish in Foil

Prepare this one ahead of time for company; when ready, just take foil packets from refrigerator and cook. Couscous would go nicely with this dish. Or rice.

1 small zucchini, thinly sliced
6-8 fresh mushrooms, sliced
1 small red onion, thinly sliced
2 6-oz (175 g) firm fish fillets
2 tablespoons olive oil
juice of 1 lemon
2 fl oz (¼ cup or 60 ml) dry white wine
salt and freshly ground black pepper
1 tablespoon shredded fresh basil (or 1 teaspoon dried)
6 black pitted olives

1. Take 2 sheets of aluminum foil 12 x 24 inches (30 x 60 cm) and fold each sheet in half to form a double thickness.
2. On the center part of each foil square brush a little oil, then arrange on it half of the ingredients: zucchini, mushrooms, fish, onion slices.
3. In a small bowl, combine olive oil, lemon juice, wine, seasonings, and basil and dribble the mixture over each arrangement. Place halved olives on top.
4. Fold the foil into airtight packets.
5. Bake in a preheated oven at 425°F (220°C) for 20-25 minutes.
6. With a spatula, carefully lift the fish and vegetables out of the foil onto individual, warmed serving plates and pour any leftover liquid over each serving.

Serves 2

Indian Prawns with Courgettes

The courgette may not be an Indian vegetable, but this recipe produces a lovely Indian dish to give your taste buds a treat. Serve with basmati rice.

2 medium-large courgettes (about 1 lb or 450 g)
5 tablespoons oil
6 cloves garlic, crushed
3 oz (75 g) chopped fresh coriander
1 hot green chili
½ teaspoon turmeric
1 ½ teaspoons cumin
¼ teaspoon cayenne
1 teaspoon finely grated fresh ginger
1 small tin of tomatoes
juice of half a lemon
salt, to taste
¾ lb (350 g) peeled prawns (shrimp)

1. Cut courgettes into strips about 2 inches (5 cm) long.
2. Heat oil in frying pan and put in the courgette strips and chopped garlic. Sauté for 2-3 minutes.
3. Add coriander, finely chopped green chili, turmeric, cumin, cayenne, ginger, finely chopped tomatoes and their liquid, lemon juice, and salt. Mix ingredients together and bring to a simmer.
4. Stir in the prawns. Cover and simmer for 3 minutes.
5. Uncover, turn heat to medium and boil away liquid to be left with a thick sauce.

Serves 4

Lamb Biryani

You have the option of omitting the lamb if you prefer to make a vegetarian dish. In any case, this simple recipe will produce a tasty Indian treat.

1 large courgette, thickly sliced
1 carrot, thickly sliced
1 large red onion, cut into wedges
1 red pepper, deseeded and cut into six segments
1 small aubergine (eggplant), thickly sliced
2 tablespoons olive oil
12 oz (350 g) chopped lamb fillet (optional)
salt and pepper
2 tablespoons mild curry paste
4 oz (125 g) basmati rice
12-16 fl oz (1½-2 cups or 360-450 ml) vegetable stock
2 tablespoons fresh coriander, chopped

1. Toss the vegetables in the oil. Spread out in a roasting pan and sprinkle with salt and freshly ground black pepper. If you opt for a lamb dish, add it to the roasting pan.
2. Cook for 20 minutes in a preheated oven at 375°F (190°C) until vegetables start to turn golden.
3. Stir in the curry paste, rice and stock and cook for another 20-30 minutes or until the liquid is absorbed and rice is tender.
4. Stir in the coriander and serve straight away.

Serves 4

Imam Bayildi

*The name of this dish is "The Priest Has Fainted"—
ostensibly because the taste was ineffable. This stuffed
aubergine recipe, while promising, does not promise to
make dinner guests faint.*

3 aubergines (eggplants)
4 tablespoons olive oil
1 large onion, chopped
½ large green pepper,
chopped
2-3 garlic cloves,
crushed
2 small-medium
courgettes, chopped
1 lb (450 g) tomatoes,
roughly chopped

1 teaspoon sugar
1 teaspoon cinnamon
4 tablespoons raisins
2 tablespoons
chopped fresh
parsley
½-1 teaspoon salt
freshly ground black
pepper

1. Cut aubergines in half lengthwise. Scoop out the flesh leaving a very thin border and chop the insides roughly.
2. Heat oil in a large frying pan and cook the onion, green pepper, and garlic for 5-10 minutes. Add the chopped aubergines and more oil if needed. Continue cooking, stirring occasionally, until aubergine is soft and lightly browned. Add the courgettes, tomatoes, sugar, cinnamon, raisins, and half the parsley. Cover and cook for a further 5 minutes. Season with salt and pepper. Remove from heat.
3. Brush the inside of the aubergine shells with oil. Spoon the mixture into the shells and sprinkle the remaining parsley over the tops. Place the shells in a shallow baking dish.
4. Bake at 350°F (180°C) for about 40 minutes. Serve warm with white rice and a green salad.

Serves 6

Mediterranean Chicken with Zucchini

A wholesome and succulent recipe to add to your healthy cuisine repertoire.

medium-size chicken, skinned and cut into sections
salt and pepper
3 medium zucchini
1 green pepper, cut into strips
1 lb (450 g) fresh mushrooms, cut into thick slices
1 small tin (10 oz or 300 ml) tomatoes, broken up
1 medium onion, chopped
2 garlic cloves, minced
2 teaspoons dried basil
1 bay leaf
Parmesan cheese (optional)

1. Sprinkle chicken with salt and pepper. Arrange pieces on a rack in a pan and bake for 10 minutes in preheated oven at 425°F (210° C). Then lower oven temperature to 350°F (180°C). Remove chicken and rack from pan and pour off any fat. Return chicken to pan.
2. Cut zucchini into 2-inch (5 cm) strips and scatter them over the chicken. Add green pepper strips and mushrooms.
3. In a large bowl, combine tomatoes, onion, garlic, basil, and bay leaf. Stir mixture well and pour over chicken.
4. Cover and bake about 50-60 minutes, or until done.
5. Sprinkle with Parmesan cheese, if desired, and serve.

Serves 4

Veal Cutlets with Zucchini

May also be prepared using chicken breast instead of veal.

6 veal cutlets
1 large egg, slightly beaten
3-4 oz (75-110 g) fine breadcrumbs
2 tablespoons olive oil
1 tin tomatoes, about 1 lb (450 g)
1 teaspoon oregano
½-1 teaspoon salt
freshly ground pepper
3 medium zucchini, sliced

1. Dip the cutlets in beaten egg, then coat in crumbs. Heat oil in pan and brown the cutlets.
2. Add the tomatoes, broken up, the oregano, salt, and a few grinds of pepper. Cover pan and simmer for 30 minutes.
3. Add sliced zucchini and cook for another 15-20 minutes.

Serves 6

Chinese Ground Beef with Zucchini and Tomatoes

*Chicken or shrimp could be substituted for the ground beef.
Serve with rice, of course.*

½ lb (225 g) ground (minced) beef
1 medium onion, sliced
3 tablespoons soy sauce
2 cloves of garlic, minced
salt and pepper, to taste
3 tablespoons oil
2 small zucchini, sliced diagonally
4 fl oz (½ cup or 120 ml) water
2 tomatoes, cut into wedges
½ teaspoon brown sugar
1 tablespoon cornstarch (corn flour) dissolved in
   2 oz (¼ cup or 60 ml) water

1. Mix ground beef, onion, soy sauce, garlic, and salt and pepper together.
2. Heat oil in wok or frying pan and stir fry ground beef mixture until browned, about 2-3 minutes.
3. Stir in zucchini and water. Cover pan and cook for five minutes, stirring two or three times. Add more water, if needed.
4. Add tomatoes and sugar. Cover and continue to cook for a further 2-3 minutes.
5. Mix together cornstarch and water and add the solution to the pan, stirring to thicken.

Serves 2-4

Accompaniments

Basic Courgettes with Fresh Herbs

This simple dish is especially good early in the season, when courgettes are young and tender and have the best flavor.

1½ lbs (700 g) young courgettes, sliced
1 oz (25 g) butter
1 tablespoon finely chopped fresh parsley
1 tablespoon finely chopped fresh chives
salt and freshly ground black pepper

1. Steam sliced courgettes for about 5 minutes until tender but not soggy.
2. Drain and add butter, herbs, and seasonings.

Serves 4-6

Sautéed Courgettes in Olive Oil

A quick and easy way to produce a good courgette dish.

1 lb (450 g) small courgettes
2 fluid oz (50 ml) olive oil
chopped parsley or basil leaves
salt and pepper

1. Cut unpeeled courgettes into ½ inch (1.2 cm) slices.
2. Sauté the slices in the olive oil in a large frying pan about 5-6 minutes until they are tender and nicely browned on each side.
3. Season with salt and pepper. Spoon into a serving dish and sprinkle with chopped parsley or basil.

Serves 4

Sautéed Zucchini with Herbs

*Seasoned with herbs, this version of sauté cooking makes
another delicious accompanying vegetable.*

**1½ lbs (700 g) zucchini
4 tablespoons olive oil
salt and pepper, to taste
2 tablespoons butter
2 garlic cloves, chopped
1 tablespoon chopped parsley
1 tablespoon chopped chives
1 tablespoon chopped dill
1 tablespoon chopped tarragon
1 tablespoon chopped fresh basil**

1. Cut unpeeled zucchini into very thin slices.
2. Add zucchini to oil that has been heated in a frying pan. Sprinkle with salt and pepper and cook over high heat, stirring gently and turning the slices over, until golden—about 5-6 minutes.
3. Add butter to the pan and, when melted, add garlic and herbs. Mix gently and serve hot.

Serves 4-6

Sautéed Courgettes with Yogurt

This could hardly be easier. Or quicker.

2 tablespoons butter
3 medium courgettes
1 medium onion, chopped
salt and freshly ground black pepper to taste
2 tablespoons chopped herbs (parsley or chives)
grated cheese (optional)
1 tablespoon yogurt

1. Cut courgettes into small cubes and sauté in butter with a chopped onion until tender. Add salt and grind in pepper to taste.
2. Sprinkle with herbs. Add grated cheese, if desired.
3. Stir in the yogurt and serve.

Serves 4-6

Turkish Courgettes with Yogurt

Unbelievably easy—as well as delicious.

4 small-medium courgettes
olive oil
salt and pepper
pinch of nutmeg
2 tablespoons chopped fresh herbs
   (parsley, basil, or mint)
8 tablespoons yogurt

1. Cut each courgette lengthwise into 4 long slices, about ½ inch (1.2 cm) thick.
2. Fry the slices in hot oil quickly, until brown, turning once.
3. Drain on paper towels and remove to serving dish.
4. Season with salt and pepper, nutmeg and herbs.
5. Spoon yogurt over and serve hot.

Serves 4

Zucchini with Tomatoes and Garlic

This is an ideal vegetable dish to serve with a main course.

6 medium zucchini
2 tablespoons butter or olive oil
2-3 cloves garlic, minced
2 tomatoes, peeled and diced
salt and pepper
2 tablespoons parsley, chopped

1. Cut unpeeled zucchini into thick rounds.
2. Heat butter or oil in a saucepan and cook garlic on low heat. Stir in the tomatoes. Add zucchini and season with salt and freshly ground pepper.
3. Cover and continue cooking on low heat for about 10-15 minutes or until zucchini is tender. Stir occasionally and add a little water if needed.
4. Sprinkle with parsley and serve.

Serves 4-6

Stuffed Courgettes

Health-conscious people can substitute curd or low-fat cheese and wholemeal breadcrumbs in this simple-to-make dish.

4 large courgettes, unpeeled
4 oz (110 g) white breadcrumbs
8 oz (225 g) cream cheese (or low-fat white cheese)
4 tablespoons flaked almonds
rind and juice of ½ lemon
salt and freshly ground black pepper

1. Boil courgettes for 4-5 minutes. Cool and slice them in half lengthwise. Remove center pulp and set aside. Arrange courgettes in a buttered baking dish.
2. In a small bowl, mix together the breadcrumbs, cheese, almonds, lemon juice and rind (to taste), and mashed courgette centers. Add salt and pepper and blend.
3. Fill the courgettes with this mixture and bake in oven preheated to 350°F (180°C) for 40-45 minutes.

Serves 4

Courgettes with Chick Pea Stuffing

This is yet another way to stuff courgettes. It can also be chilled and served in Middle Eastern style with yogurt.

4 medium-large courgettes
½ oz (15 g) butter
1 onion, chopped
2 garlic cloves, crushed
8-10 mushrooms, sliced
about 4 oz (110 g) chickpeas
1-2 teaspoons ground coriander
2 tablespoons lemon juice
2 tablespoons chopped parsley
salt and freshly ground black pepper, to taste

1. Cut unpeeled courgettes in half lengthwise. Remove center pulp, chop, and set aside. Arrange courgette shells in a buttered baking dish.
2. Melt the butter in a pan, and sauté the onion and garlic for 5 minutes, then add the chopped courgette centers and the sliced mushrooms and cook for another 5 minutes.
3. Add drained chickpeas, ground coriander, lemon juice, parsley, and salt and pepper. Blend well and fill the courgette shells with the mixture.
4. Bake in oven preheated to 350°F (180°C) about 30 minutes, or until courgettes are tender.

Serves 4

Courgettes with Parmesan Cheese

*Walnuts and cheese contribute to an interesting blend of
flavors.*

**8 small courgettes
butter
2 garlic cloves, minced
finely chopped parsley
grated Parmesan cheese
2 tablespoons chopped walnuts
salt and freshly ground black pepper**

1. Cut courgettes in half lengthwise. Dot each open half with
   butter, garlic, parsley, cheese and chopped walnuts. Sprinkle
   with salt and pepper.
2. Grill for a few minutes, allowing the top to cook while the
   courgettes remain crisp and partially uncooked.

Serves 4

Zucchini with Apricots

This is a delightful Middle-Eastern dish.

**6 small zucchini (about 2 lbs or nearly 1 kg), cut into
  ¼-inch (1.6 cm) rounds
3 tablespoons olive oil
8 oz (225 g) small dried apricots
8 fl oz (1 cup or 240 ml) water
2 tablespoons lemon juice
1 tablespoon brown sugar
salt and pepper**

1. Boil the water in a small saucepan and add apricots. Cover and simmer about 15 minutes until apricots are tender. Add sugar and lemon juice. Set aside.
2. Heat oil in a pan and sauté the zucchini over medium heat for 5 minutes, stirring frequently. Add salt and pepper.
3. Pour the apricot mixture, undrained, over the zucchini. Cook, covered, about 5 minutes until the zucchini are tender but still crisp.
4. If a thicker sauce is desired, stir a tablespoon of cornstarch (cornflour) with 2 tablespoons of water and add to pan, cooking for a minute or two until the sauce thickens.

8 servings

Sweet and Sour Courgettes

With an intriguing hint of cinnamon, this recipe is good served with grilled meat, roast chicken, or turkey.

2 lbs (1 kg) courgettes
2 tablespoons olive oil
salt and freshly ground black pepper
½ teaspoon cinnamon
4 tablespoons white wine vinegar
1 tablespoon sugar
2 tablespoons water

1. Sauté sliced, unpeeled courgettes gently in olive oil until nearly tender, about 8-10 minutes.
2. Season with salt and black pepper and cinnamon. Add wine vinegar and sugar.
3. Stir gently, turning courgettes over until the liquid is reduced to a smaller amount and the courgettes absorb the flavors, making certain that the courgettes are not overcooked.

Serves 4-6

Sicilian Style Sweet and Sour Zucchini

The Southern Italy version of sweet and sour courgettes.

2 lbs (1 kg) zucchini
2 large cloves garlic, crushed
3 tablespoons olive oil
3 tablespoons red wine vinegar
2 tablespoons water
1 oz (25 g) raisins or sultanas
1 oz (25 g) pine kernels
8 anchovy fillets
salt and freshly ground black pepper

1. Heat the oil in a large frying pan and sauté garlic. Add zucchini, cut into strips 2-3 inches (5-8 cm) long, and stir gently until they turn golden.
2. Add vinegar and water. Cover and simmer for 10-12 minutes.
3. Add raisins, pine kernels, and anchovies (rinsed of any salt or oil and chopped) and cook uncovered, until the liquid is reduced.
4. Add salt and pepper and stir to steep zucchini in the flavors of the sauce.

Serves 4-6

Zucchini Strips with Mint

This unusual way of preparing zucchini takes only about ten minutes. It makes a good accompaniment to many main courses, especially lamb.

4 small zucchini (1 lb or 450 g), peeled
1 tablespoon olive oil
2 garlic cloves, minced
pinch of salt
2 tablespoons chopped fresh mint

1. Slice the zucchini into very thin long strips with a potato peeler.
2. In a frying pan, sauté garlic in oil over medium heat for a minute or two.
3. Raise heat to high and add zucchini strips and salt. Cook and stir until zucchini wilts—about 2 minutes.
4. Remove from heat and stir in mint.

Serves 4

Courgettes and Carrots à la Menthe

Colorful and easy.

3 carrots, sliced into ¼ inch (less than 1 cm) rounds
2 medium courgettes, sliced into ¼ inch (less than 1 cm)
 rounds
2 tablespoons butter
salt and freshly ground pepper
2 teaspoons fresh mint, chopped

1. Heat butter in a heavy frying pan and cook the sliced carrots in it, covered, for about 4-5 minutes.
2. Add sliced courgettes. Sprinkle with salt and pepper to taste. Cover and cook another 4-5 minutes, stirring occasionally, until vegetables are tender. Sprinkle with mint.

4 servings

Dijon Carrots and Zucchini

This fatless recipe blends mustard and other ingredients and carrots to give the zucchini a sweet and savory flavor.

2-3 medium zucchini cut into 2-inch (5 cm) sticks
2 medium-large carrots cut into 2-inch (5 cm) sticks
2 tablespoons chicken broth
1 teaspoon apple cider vinegar
1 teaspoon honey
1 ½ teaspoons Dijon mustard
salt and pepper to taste

1. Cut zucchini into 2-inch (5 cm) sticks and set aside.
2. Cut carrots into 2-inch (5 cm) sticks and cook them in the broth in a covered saucepan over medium heat for 10 minutes.
3. Add zucchini and cook for another 5 minutes or until vegetables are tender, adding more broth if necessary.
4. Mix vinegar, honey and mustard together and stir the mixture into the vegetables. Add salt and pepper.
5. Cook for a few more minutes until liquid evaporates.

4 servings

Poor Person's Zucchini

There is nothing poor about this healthy regional dish which derives its name from the fact that in southern Italy (Apulia) the ingredients would be inexpensive or readily available from the garden.

8 small-medium zucchini
6 tablespoons olive oil
1 bunch of fresh mint, coarsely chopped
8 tablespoons red wine vinegar
2-3 large cloves garlic, chopped
pinch of salt (optional)

1. Slice the zucchini lengthwise into thin strips.
2. Heat the oil, and fry zucchini and chopped garlic for about 4-5 minutes, turning the strips over, until golden. Drain on paper towels.
3. Arrange in layers in a serving dish or casserole and sprinkle with half the mint.
4. Measure wine vinegar into a pan, adding salt (if desired) and remaining mint. Bring to the boil, then simmer for about 5 minutes. Pour the hot marinade all over the zucchini.
5. Allow to cool. Serve slightly chilled.

Serves 6-8

Lemon Zucchini

Another simple recipe that is simply good.

4 small zucchini
2 tablespoons butter
2 tablespoons lemon juice
½ teaspoon grated lemon rind
salt and pepper to taste
chopped parsley

1. Cut zucchini into ¼-inch (.6 cm) slices. Cook uncovered in boiling water for 3-4 minutes, or steam. Drain.
2. Heat butter, lemon juice and lemon rind in a small saucepan, stirring until butter is melted. Season with salt and pepper. Pour over the zucchini. Garnish with parsley.

4 servings

Zucchini with Oil and Lemon

Another way to use lemon with zucchini.

3 large zucchini
3 tablespoons olive oil
salt and pepper
juice of half a lemon

1. Cut zucchini into quarters, then into two-inch (5 cm) lengths.
2. Heat oil in a frying pan and add zucchini; sprinkle with salt and pepper to taste. Cook until they turn golden.
3. Add lemon juice. Cover and cook about 3 minutes, until crisp.

4 servings

Grated Courgettes with Lemon Juice

Lemon again, but with a very different effect.

2 large courgettes (about 1 lb or 500 g)
juice of 1 lemon
salt and pepper, to taste
1 teaspoon fresh tarragon or basil
2 oz (50 g) butter

1. Grate courgettes finely and mix with fresh lemon juice.
2. Add salt and pepper and tarragon or basil. Refrigerate for at least 5 hours.
3. When ready to serve, sauté the mixture in heated butter for about 4 minutes.

Serves 4-6

Zucchini à l'Orange

This may be prepared in advance and refrigerated. When ready to serve, simmer until heated through.

2 lbs (nearly 1 kg) zucchini, sliced into rounds
3 oz (80 g) butter
salt and pepper
2 tablespoons orange juice
1 tablespoon grated orange rind

1. Sauté thinly-sliced zucchini in butter until just tender.
2. Season with salt and pepper
3. Remove from heat. Add orange juice and orange rind and mix together.

Serves 6

Zucchini Fans

Cutting zucchini into fan shapes makes such an attractive presentation that people will think you put in a lot more effort than this surprisingly easy—as well as tasty—recipe actually calls for.

4 small zucchini (about 4-5 oz or 125 g each)
salt and pepper
a little flour
2 tablespoons butter

1. Trim zucchini and slice them lengthwise into a fan shape, cutting up to ¾ inch (2 cm) of the stalk end, to hold the slices together.
2. Open out the fan. Sprinkle with salt and pepper. Dip the zucchini fans into flour and shake off any excess.
3. Heat butter in a large skillet and fry for 5 minutes on each side. Add more butter if needed.

Serves 4

Marrow in Tomato and Coriander Sauce

Next time you have an overgrown courgette, try cooking it in this tomato sauce recipe for a spicy and delicious result.

1 marrow (about 1½-2 lbs or 700-900 g)
1 onion, chopped
2 tablespoons olive oil
2 tablespoons tomato paste (purée)
2 teaspoons coriander seeds, coarsely crushed
1 teaspoon green peppercorns
salt and freshly ground black pepper
½ teaspoon sugar (optional)

1. Peel marrow and cut into small cubes.
2. Sauté onion in oil in a pan for 5 minutes.
3. Add marrow, tomato paste, coriander, green peppercorns, salt and pepper. Mix.
4. Cover and simmer gently for about 15 minutes until marrow is nearly tender. Then boil uncovered for 5-10 minutes until liquid has evaporated.
5. Adjust seasonings and add sugar, if needed.

Serves 4

Spicy Ginger Marrow

This savory recipe can also be made with smaller zucchini.

1 marrow, about 1½-2 lbs (700-900 g)
1 medium onion, chopped
2 tablespoons olive oil
1-2 teaspoons ground ginger
2 oz (50 g) stem ginger, chopped
salt and pepper
fresh parsley, chopped

1. Peel marrow and cut into small cubes. It is not necessary to remove seeds if tender.
2. Heat oil in a pan and sauté onion for 5 minutes. Add marrow together with ground and chopped ginger.
3. Cook gently in covered pan until marrow is nearly tender, about 15 minutes.
4. Then uncover and allow to boil for 5-10 minutes until liquid has evaporated.
5. Season with salt and pepper to taste and sprinkle with chopped parsley before serving.

Serves 4

Mexican Courgettes and Corn in Tomato Sauce

Courgettes or **calabacitas** *are basic to a Mexican diet and are often added to sauces. This excellent side dish uses a method of charring and skinning vegetables, popular in Mexico, that imparts a sweet and smoky flavor.*

4 ripe tomatoes, charred and peeled
½ green chili, charred
1 clove garlic, charred
½ onion, charred
2 teaspoons oil
4 fl oz (120 ml) water
4 courgettes, cubed
4 oz (110 g) fresh or frozen corn kernels
¼ teaspoon salt
pinch of freshly ground black pepper

1. Skin tomatoes, chili, garlic and onion by charring them under the grill or in a hot and heavy frying pan. Turn frequently until black and blistered, and peel when cool enough to handle.
2. Purée the vegetables in a blender or food processor.
3. Heat the oil in a saucepan and cook the purée for 3 minutes, stirring continually.
4. Add the water, courgettes, corn, salt and pepper, and simmer for about 10 minutes. Serve hot.

Serves 4

Puebla Style Courgettes

*This adaptation of a Mexican recipe for **calabacitas**, or courgettes, substitutes green peppers for **poblano**, a local green pepper used in **mole poblano**, the famous dish of the state of Puebla. Sweet green peppers will also yield excellent results for this unusual vegetable dish that goes well with any plain meat, poultry, or fish. You can also vary it by topping with slices of cheese such as Spanish **queso blanco** or mild Cheddar to make an attractive vegetarian lunch dish.*

3 sweet green peppers, toasted, peeled, and seeded
1 medium onion, chopped
1 clove garlic, chopped
3 tablespoons vegetable oil
1 lb (450 g) small courgettes, cut into ½ inch (1.2 cm)
   cubes
4 fl oz (120 ml) water
salt and pepper
5 tablespoons heavy cream

1. Chop the toasted, peeled, and seeded peppers coarsely and purée them in a food processor with the onion and garlic.
2. Heat the oil in a saucepan and sauté the purée, stirring constantly for about 3-4 minutes. Add the courgettes, and season to taste with salt and pepper.
3. Add a little water, about half a cup (or 4 fl oz). Cover and simmer until the courgettes are tender, about 20 minutes. Add more water, if needed. (There should be just enough liquid to cook the courgettes.)
4. Stir in the cream and simmer, uncovered, just long enough to heat it through.

Serves 4-6

Courgette Rice

Any leftovers are also delicious served cold, as a salad. It may also be frozen.

2 tablespoons olive oil
2 onions, chopped
2 large garlic cloves, crushed
1 large red pepper, chopped
1½ lb (700 g) courgettes, sliced
6 oz (175 g) brown rice
14 oz (400 g) tin tomatoes
salt and freshly ground black pepper
2 tablespoons chopped parsley

1. Sauté the onions and garlic in the oil for 5 minutes, until golden. Add pepper and cook for another 3-4 minutes.
2. Add the rice and courgettes, stirring to coat them with oil.
3. Add the tomatoes and salt and pepper.
4. Bring to a boil, then reduce heat. Cover and simmer gently over low heat for 40 minutes. There should be enough liquid from the vegetables for cooking the rice. Otherwise, add water.
5. Remove pan from heat, stir mixture, and allow to stand, covered, for about 10 minutes.
6. Adjust seasonings. Sprinkle with parsley and serve.

Serves 6

Farfalle with Courgettes, Peas, and Mint

Farfalle are pasta in the shape of bow ties or butterflies. Of course, you can use other shapes such as ribbons or fettuccine.

8-12 oz (225-350 g) farfalle
1 oz (25 g) butter
1 tablespoon olive oil
1 lb (450 g) courgettes, thinly sliced
6 oz (175 g) shelled peas
2 tablespoons chopped mint
salt and freshly ground black pepper
grated Parmesan cheese

1. Cook pasta in boiling water until just tender. Drain.
2. Meanwhile, cook the courgettes and peas in melted butter and oil over low heat for about 6-8 minutes.
3. Turn courgettes and peas, together with pan juices, into a hot serving dish. Add hot, drained pasta and chopped mint. Gently mix it all together, adding salt and a few grinds of pepper.
4. Sprinkle with grated Parmesan cheese and serve.

Serves 4-6

Baked Courgettes with Goat Cheese

Other cheeses such as cheddar or mozzarella may be substituted.

8 small courgettes, unpeeled
2 tablespoons olive oil
3-4 oz (about 80-110 g) goat cheese
fresh mint, finely chopped
freshly ground black pepper

1. Cut a thin slit lengthwise in each courgette.
2. Insert strips of goat cheese into slits. Add mint and a few grinds of pepper. Sprinkle with 1 tablespoon of the oil.
3. Wrap each courgette in a rectangle of aluminum foil that has been brushed with the remaining oil.
4. Bake in preheated oven at 350°F (180°C) for about 20-25 minutes.

Serves 4

Courgette and Cheese Gratin

Pungent feta cheese takes away any blandness attributed to courgettes, but you may substitute for it an equal mixture of cottage cheese and grated Parmesan.

3 large courgettes
1 lb (450 g) feta cheese
3 eggs, lightly beaten
salt and pepper to taste
pinch of nutmeg
4-5 sprigs of fresh mint or 3 teaspoons dried mint

1. Cut courgettes into thick slices. Boil for a few minutes, until just tender but still crisp and drain. Arrange them closely together in a lightly-greased shallow baking dish.
2. Mash the feta with a fork and add the rest of the ingredients. Stir well and spoon the mixture over the courgettes.
3. Bake in a preheated 350°F (180°C) oven for about 30 minutes, until the top is lightly browned.
4. Serve hot or cold. May be served with yogurt.

Serves 6-8

Grilled Garlic Zucchini

Zucchini is an excellent vegetable choice for grilling on your outdoor barbecue. Mix green and yellow ones, if you have them, for an even more colorful effect.

6 medium-large zucchini, cut in half lengthwise
2 cloves garlic, crushed
1 tablespoon olive oil
juice of half a lemon
1 ½ teaspoons basil
salt and pepper

1. Mix together garlic, oil, lemon juice, and seasonings. Brush cut surfaces of zucchini with half of this garlic mixture.
2. Place on preheated grill, cut side down, and grill for 4 minutes.
3. Turn and brush with remaining garlic mixture and cook for another 4 minutes or until tender.

6 servings

Baked Zucchini Sticks

This attractive and delicious vegetable recipe can be served topped with tomato sauce.

1 lb (450 g) zucchini
3 tablespoons wheat germ
¼ teaspoon garlic powder
½ teaspoon paprika
1 teaspoon oregano
salt and pepper to taste

1. Cut 2 large unpeeled zucchini lengthwise into eighths —
    or 4 small zucchini lengthwise into quarters.
2. Combine remaining ingredients in a small bowl. Mix well and
    spread onto a plate.
3. Press cut sides of zucchini into the mixture so that the crumbs
    stick.
4. Arrange zucchini, cut sides up, on a lightly oiled baking sheet.
    Any leftover crumbs can be sprinkled over the top.
5. Bake in preheated 400° F (200°C) oven for 15 minutes, until
    tender but still crisp.

4 servings

Baked Zucchini with Tomatoes

Makes a colorful presentation.

2 medium zucchini
4 medium tomatoes
1 green pepper, chopped
l medium onion, chopped
salt and pepper to taste
3-4 tablespoons olive oil

1. Cut zucchini and tomatoes into slices. Arrange them in a lightly-buttered baking dish, alternating and slightly overlapping the zucchini and tomato slices.
2. Scatter green pepper, onion, salt and pepper over the top and sprinkle with oil.
3. Bake in hot oven at 400°F (200°C) for about 20-25 minutes.

Serves 2-4

Roasted Summer Vegetables

Baked vegetables are easy and delicious, and this method prevents them from drying out. Substitutions or additions such as carrots or strips of red pepper can yield an even greater color medley for this attractive dish which goes well with roast chicken or grilled meat or fish.

6 baby zucchini
6 baby eggplants (aubergines)
1 lb (450 g) green beans
6 new potatoes
4 fl oz (½ cup or 120 ml) olive oil
salt

1. Arrange vegetables close together to fill a shallow baking dish in a single layer.
2. Sprinkle with olive oil and salt.
3. Bake in oven preheated to 375°F (190°C) until brown and wilted. Since cooking times vary for different vegetables, remove them as they become tender – about 30 minutes for zucchini and eggplant, perhaps an hour for potatoes – and arrange them on a serving plate.
4. Serve at room temperature for maximum flavor.

6 servings

Cheese-Stuffed Zucchini

Another way to appreciate stuffed courgettes as an accompanying vegetable.

6 small zucchini
2 oz (50 g) grated Parmesan cheese
1 egg
3 oz (80 g) fine breadcrumbs
salt and pepper to taste
2 tomatoes, coarsely chopped

1. Slice each zucchini in half lengthwise and parboil them. Remove center pulp and set aside.
2. Mix together the cheese, egg, and breadcrumbs. Season with salt and pepper. Use this mixture to fill each zucchini half.
3. Place the pulp and tomato pieces in a baking dish, and arrange the filled zucchini halves on top.
4. Cover and cook in a low oven, 325°F (160°C) for 40-45 minutes.

Serves 6

Vermouth Zucchini with Onions

If you have no vermouth, use dry sherry instead.

6 tablespoons dry vermouth
6 small-medium zucchinis, thinly sliced
l large onion, chopped
1 tablespoon fresh thyme (or 1 teaspoon dried)
salt
freshly ground black pepper

1. In a large frying pan, heat 3 tablespoons of vermouth.
2. Add all the other ingredients and cook over medium heat for about 7 minutes, stirring occasionally. Add the remaining vermouth when mixture starts becoming dry. Cover and cook about 15 minutes, until zucchini is tender but still crisp.
3. Taste for seasonings and serve.

4-6 servings

Curried Zucchini

*If you like curry, here's an easy recipe for your repertory.
Moreover, you can use it for any vegetable.*

3 tablespoons olive oil
1-2 cloves garlic, minced
1 medium onion, chopped
salt and pepper to taste
2 teaspoons curry powder
pinch of red or cayenne pepper (optional)
3 medium zucchini, sliced
2 tomatoes, cut into small pieces

1. In a large frying pan, sauté garlic and onion in olive oil until soft.
2. Add salt and pepper, curry powder—and red pepper, if desired. Mix well.
3. Add the zucchini and cook until tender, about 8-10 minutes.
4. Stir in tomatoes, adjust seasonings, and serve.

Serves 4-6

Southwestern Zucchini with Corn and Green Chiles

*Since chiles, basic to the cooking style of the American
Southwest, vary greatly in both size and taste, check intensity to
make sure the type you use is not too hot for your taste.*

2 oz (¼ cup or 50 g) butter
1 tablespoon olive oil
1 medium onion, chopped
4 oz (½ cup or 100 g) chopped fresh green chiles
4 small-medium zucchinis, cut into ½-inch (1.2 cm) slices
**12-16 oz (1½-2 cups or 350 g-450 g) fresh (or frozen) corn
  kernels**
¼ teaspoon dried oregano
¼ teaspoon cumin
½ teaspoon salt
4 fl oz (½ cup or 120 ml) chicken stock

1. In a frying pan, heat butter and olive oil. Sauté onion and
    green chile for about 3 minutes.
2. Add zucchini, corn (cut from about 4 ears), oregano, cumin,
    and salt. Mix well.
3. Add stock. Cover and simmer for about 5 minutes, until
    zucchini is tender and crisp.

Serves 6

Bread and Cake

Zucchini Bread

As this recipe makes two loaves, keep one in the freezer for emergency use. You can also store chopped zucchini in measured quantities in the freezer, ready for baking in those off-season months when zucchini is not available from your garden.

3 eggs, beaten
4 oz (½ cup or 110 g) granulated sugar
5 oz (140 g) brown sugar
4 fl oz (½ cup or 120 ml) sunflower oil
3 teaspoons maple flavoring
2 zucchini, coarsely chopped (2 cups, about 1 lb or 450 g)
2 teaspoons baking soda (bicarbonate of soda)
½ teaspoon baking powder
½ teaspoon salt
4 oz (½ cup or 110 g) wheat germ
20 oz (2½ cups or 550 g) flour
4 oz (½ cup or 110 g) walnuts, chopped
4-6 tablespoons sesame seeds

1. Beat eggs. Add sugars, oil and maple flavoring and beat all together until thick and foamy. Stir in zucchini.
2. Add baking soda, baking powder, salt, wheat germ and flour. Mix well. Blend in the walnuts.
3. Turn batter into two greased 9 x 5 inch (23 x 13 cm) loaf pans. Sprinkle sesame seeds over tops.
4. Bake in preheated oven at 350°F (180°C) for 45-55 minutes or until a toothpick inserted into center comes out clean.

Yields 2 loaves, 12 slices each

Zucchini Spice Bread

*Here's another good cake for your afternoon tea
repertory, or for any occasion.*

8 oz (1 cup or 225 g)
white flour
8 oz (2 cups or 225 g)
whole wheat flour
¼ teaspoon salt
2 ½ teaspoons baking
powder
¼ teaspoon nutmeg
½ teaspoon allspice
½ teaspoon cinnamon
½ teaspoon ginger
4 fl oz (½ cup or 120 ml)

honey
6 tablespoons melted
butter
2 eggs
½ teaspoon vanilla
2 zucchini, coarsely
grated (2 cups,
about 1 lb or 450 g)
4 oz (½ cup or 110 g)
chopped nuts
4 oz (½ cup or 110 g)
raisins (optional)

1. Sift flours into a bowl together with salt, baking powder, nutmeg, allspice, cinnamon, ginger, and set aside.
2. In a large bowl, beat the honey at high speed until it is opaque. Beat in the butter, eggs, and vanilla, continuing to beat for a few more minutes.
3. Add dry ingredients to the mixture alternately with the zucchini, beginning and ending with the dry ingredients. Blend after each addition.
4. Stir in nuts and raisins.
5. Pour into a buttered, medium-size loaf pan about 10 x 6 inches (25 x 15 cm).
6. Bake 30-35 minutes in preheated oven at 350°F (180°C) until toothpick inserted into center comes out clean.

Makes 1 loaf, about 16 slices
Makes 1 loaf, about 16 slices

Zucchini Pineapple Bread

This bread is more like cake and excellent served at afternoon tea.

3 eggs
8 fl oz (1 cup or 240 ml) vegetable oil
16 oz (2 cups or 450g) sugar (or less)
1 teaspoon vanilla
2 unpeeled medium zucchini, shredded (about 1 lb
  or 450 g)
1 can crushed pineapple, drained (about 20 oz or 550 g)
1 lb (3 cups or 450 g) flour
2 teaspoons baking soda (bicarbonate of soda)
½ teaspoon baking powder
1½ teaspoons cinnamon
¾ teaspoon nutmeg
1 teaspoon salt
8 oz (225 g) finely chopped walnuts
8 oz (225 g) raisins

1. Combine eggs, vegetable oil, sugar, and vanilla in a large bowl and beat until thick and foamy.
2. Mix in zucchini and drained pineapple.
3. Add sifted flour and the rest of the ingredients. Blend well.
4. Spoon batter into two greased 9 x 5 inch (23 x 13 cm) loaf pans. Bake in preheated oven at 350°F (180°C) 55 to 60 minutes or until toothpick inserted in the center comes out clean.

Yield: 2 loaves

Zucchini Muffins

This is a healthy muffin that is low in cholesterol—and delicious.

5 oz (1 cup or 140 g) whole wheat flour
5 oz (1 cup or 140 g) white flour
2 teaspoons baking soda (bicarbonate of soda)
¼ teaspoon baking powder
1 tablespoon cinnamon
1 egg
4 fl oz (½ cup or 120 ml) sunflower oil
6 oz (175 g) sugar (or less)
4 oz (100 g) nonfat dry milk
3 zucchini, grated (2½ cups or about 1½ lbs or 550 g)
2 teaspoons vanilla
1 tablespoon lemon juice
4 oz (½ cup or 110 g) raisins
3 oz (80 g) chopped walnuts

1. Mix together flours, baking soda, baking powder and cinnamon. Set aside.
2. In another bowl beat together egg, oil, and sugar. Add powdered milk, grated zucchini, vanilla and lemon juice and beat thoroughly.
3. Add flour mixture and mix until smooth.
4. Stir in raisins and walnuts.
5. Spoon into greased muffin cups, two-thirds full. Bake in preheated oven at 350°C (180°F) for 15-20 minutes.

Makes 2 dozen muffins

Carrot and Courgette Cake

The grated carrot-courgette combination is the basis for an excellent cake.

8 oz (225 g) flour
2 teaspoons baking powder
1 teaspoon baking soda (bicarbonate of soda)
1 teaspoon salt 8 oz (225 g) sugar
1 oz (25 g) pine nuts
1 oz (25 g) sultanas or raisins
2 mashed ripe bananas
3 eggs, beaten
8 oz (225 g) mixed carrots and courgettes, grated

5 fl oz (150 ml) sunflower oil

Frosting:
 5 oz (140 g) cream cheese
4 oz (110 g) softened butter
½ teaspoon vanilla
8 oz (225 g) icing sugar

1. Sift flour into a large bowl and add baking powder, baking soda, and salt. Mix in sugar, pine nuts and sultanas.
2. Add mashed bananas and beaten eggs. Stir in the grated carrots and courgettes. Add the oil and beat thoroughly for a minute to obtain a thick and slightly lumpy mixture.
3. Spoon the batter into a greased 9-inch (23 cm) cake tin, preferably spring form, and bake in preheated oven at 350°F (180°C) for 50-60 minutes, or until a toothpick inserted into the center comes out clean. Let stand for a few minutes before removing cake from the tin.
4. To make the frosting, beat cream cheese, butter and vanilla until smooth. Gradually add sugar, beating after each addition. Allow icing to stand for a while until it is of right consistency to spread.

Wholemeal Courgette and Raisin Cake

*Good eaten plain, this moist cake may also be spread with
cream cheese frosting.*

7 oz (200 g) wholemeal flour
1 teaspoon baking soda (bicarbonate of soda)
2 teaspoons baking powder
1 teaspoon salt
1 teaspoon ground ginger
8 oz (1 cup or 225 g) brown sugar
4 oz (½ cup or 110 g) raisins
1 medium courgette (8 oz or 225 g), grated
2 oz (50 g) grated carrot
7 oz (200 g) crushed pineapple, drained
8 fl oz (1 cup or 240 ml) plain yogurt
3 large eggs, beaten
2 fl oz (150 ml) sunflower oil

1. Put flour, baking soda, baking powder, salt, ginger, sugar and raisins in a large mixing bowl. Stir in the grated courgettes and carrots and the drained pineapple.
2. Add the yogurt, eggs, and oil.
3. Beat thoroughly for 1 minute to yield a thick batter.
4. Scrape the batter into a greased 9-inch (23 cm) round cake tin and bake in preheated 350°F (180°C) oven for 1 hour, until a toothpick inserted into the center comes out clean. Cool slightly before turning out.

Chocolate Courgette Layer Cake

Perhaps an unlikely combination, but you're in for a yummy surprise. So are friends, who will never guess the secret ingredient.

4 oz (110 g) butter
6 tablespoons sugar
2 eggs
3 oz (80 g) baking chocolate
2 tablespoons clear honey
5 oz (1 cup or 140 g) flour
2 tablespoons unsweetened cocoa
1½ teaspoons baking powder
4 fl oz (½ cup or 140 ml) milk
1 teaspoon vanilla
1 medium courgette, grated

Frosting:
2 oz (50 g) plain chocolate
3 tablespoons water
2 tablespoons butter
8 oz (225 g) confectioner's (icing) sugar, sifted

1. Cream together butter and sugar until light and fluffy. Beat in the eggs.
2. Stir chocolate and honey in a small bowl over a pan of hot water until the chocolate has melted. Cool. Then beat the chocolate mixture into the butter, sugar, and eggs.
3. Sift together flour, cocoa, and baking powder. Stir in the flour mixture, a little at a time, alternating with milk and vanilla.

4. Stir in grated courgette and mix well.

5. Pour the mixture into two greased 7 ½ inch (18-19 cm) cake tins.

6. Bake in pre-heated oven at 350° F (180° C) oven for about 30-35 minutes, until a toothpick inserted in the center comes out clean.

7. For frosting, melt the chocolate and water in a small saucepan over low heat. Remove from heat and stir in butter until it melts. Beat in the sugar. Spread over cake.

Chocolate Zucchini Cake

Although the zucchini is a subtle ingredient in this recipe, it yields a moist and flavorful cake.

4 oz (110 g) butter
4 fl oz (½ cup or 120 ml) sunflower oil
4 oz (½ cup or 110 g) granulated sugar
5 oz (1 cup or 140 g) brown sugar
3 eggs
4 fl oz (½ cup or 120 ml) sour cream or yogurt
1 teaspoon vanilla
12 oz (2½ cups or 340-350 g) plain flour
2 teaspoons baking powder
4 tablespoons unsweetened cocoa
½ teaspoon ground allspice
l lb (450 g) courgettes, peeled and grated
about 8 oz (1 cup or 225 g) chocolate chips
chopped walnuts (optional)

1. Cream the butter, oil and sugars together until light and fluffy. Then gradually beat in the eggs.
2. Add sour cream and vanilla and mix well.
3. Sift the flour into a bowl and add baking powder, cocoa, and allspice. Gently blend dry ingredients into the creamed mixture.
4. Stir in the grated courgettes and blend well. Add walnuts if desired.
5. Spread the batter evenly into a greased 9 x 13 inch (23 x 31 cm) greased baking tin. Sprinkle chocolate chips over the top.
6. Bake for 40-45 minutes in a preheated oven at 350°F (180°C) until the cake is firm and a toothpick inserted in the center comes out clean. Cut into squares while still warm.

Courgette Bread Loaf

Although the addition of grated courgettes will keep the bread fresh longer, this loaf is too good to be kept for very long.

1 lb (450 g) courgettes, coursely grated
1 ¼ lbs (4 cups or 550 g) plain flour
2 teaspoons yeast
4 tablespoons fresh Parmesan cheese, grated
black pepper to taste
2 tablespoons olive oil
water
milk
sesame seeds

1. Grate the courgettes and set aside in a colander to drain for 30 minutes. Pat dry.
2. Mix flour, yeast, Parmesan cheese, and pepper.
3. Add the courgettes and oil. Mix together and add enough lukewarm water to make a firm dough.
4. Knead on a floured board until smooth. Put it back in the mixing bowl, cover, and allow to rise in a warm place until the size has doubled.
5. Remove dough and knead lightly. Then place it in a greased loaf tin. Brush the top with milk and sprinkle with sesame seeds. Allow it to rise again.
6. Bake in a preheated oven at 400°F (200°C) for 25 minutes or until brown and done.

Random Recipes
for
Rotund Marrows

Marrow Ginger Jam

As marrows become larger, they also become filled with water rather than flavor. Huge marrows are prized by horticultural show judges who do not have to eat them.This is an unusual solution for using up good courgettes that have swelled into bulging marrows, perhaps while you were away on holiday.

4 lbs (2 kg) prepared marrow cubes
3 lbs (1 ½ kg) preserving sugar
1 oz (30 g) root ginger
3 large lemons, thinly peeled rind and juice

1. Prepare marrows by peeling and seeding them, then cutting into cubes.
2. Sprinkle with a third of the sugar and allow to stand overnight.
3. Pound the ginger with a mallet to crush the hard fibrous flesh and to allow flavor to escape.
4. Place ginger and lemon rind in a muslin bag and tie the bag.
5. Put marrow and its juices into a large pot. Add the remaining sugar, the lemon juice and the muslin bag.
6. Cook slowly, making sure sugar is dissolved before the boiling point is reached. Continue to boil steadily until marrow looks transparent. Taste after 15 minutes to adjust flavor, and remove bag if mixture is strong enough. Cook until the setting point is reached.

Stuffed Marrow Rings

Here is a recipe to appreciate when you are 'stuck' with an overgrown, show-size marrow. The Mediterranean rice stuffing will absorb the water and work better than a breadcrumb stuffing which may become soggy.

1 marrow
1 medium onion, chopped
1-2 garlic cloves, chopped
4 fl oz (½ cup or 120 ml) olive oil
8 oz (250 g) rice
1 tablespoon tomato paste (optional)
5 fl oz (150 ml) water
1 tablespoon mint, chopped
1 tablespoon dill weed, chopped
¼ teaspoon ground cinnamon
salt and pepper to taste

1. Cut the large marrow across into rings, about 1 inch (nearly 3 cm) thick. Remove the seeds in the center and blanch the rings for 5 minutes. Arrange the rings in a buttered baking dish.
2. To make the stuffing, heat the oil in a saucepan and sauté the onion and garlic until soft but not browned. Stir in the rice, tomato paste, and water. Simmer for 5 minutes.
3. Add the rest of the ingredients. Remove from heat and season to taste.
4. Fill marrow centers with the stuffing, allowing it to spill over and form a rounded shape.
5. Bake in 375°F (190°C) oven for 45-60 minutes. Serve, allowing one or two rounds per person.

And More Marrows. . . .

Don't forget these recipes for marrows, which have appeared in previous sections.

TABLE OF WEIGHTS AND MEASURES

COURGETTES/ZUCCHINI
small courgette = up to 5-6 oz (140-175 g)
medium courgette = 6-8 oz (175-225 g)
large courgette = over 8 oz (225 g)

TEASPOON AND TABLESPOON MEASUREMENTS ARE
LEVEL

LIQUID EQUIVALENTS
1 litre = 1000 ml = 1 ¾ Imperial pints = 2 US pints = 4 cups
     600 ml = 1 Imperial pint = 1 ¼ US pint = 2 ½ cups
½ litre = 500 ml = ¾ Imperial pint = 1 US pint = 2 cups
     300 ml = ½ Imperial pint = 1 ¼ cups
¼ litre = 250 ml = 8 fl oz = ½ US pint = 1 cup
     150 ml = 5 fl oz = 2/3 cup
     100-125 ml = 3 ½ - 4 fl oz = 1/3 - ½ cup

WEIGHTS
28 g = 1 oz
110 g = 4 oz or ½ cup
225 g = 8 oz or 1 cup
450 g = 16 oz or 1 lb
1 kg = 2 lbs

SOME INGREDIENT MEASUREMENTS
fresh breadcrumbs 3 ½ oz (100 g) = 2 cups
butter   8 oz (250 g) = 1 cup
cheese, grated   2 oz (50-60 g) = ½ cup
flour   1 lb (500 g) = 3 ¾ cups
               5 oz (150 g) = 1 cup
sugar   2 oz (50-60 g) = 1/3 cup

COMMENTS ON COURGETTES

The word courgette is a diminutive of the French *courge*, meaning marrow. Zucchini means miniature *zucca*, or gourd, in Italian.

Calabacitas are courgettes in Spain or Mexico.

The courgette is classified as a summer squash, *cucurbita pepo*, together with marrows and little pattypan squashes.

Courgettes, bushier than other plants in the family, grow over the ground and readily adapt themselves to many soil types.

Courgettes have a long growing season and are satisfying to cultivate as they grow in abundance; the more they are picked, the more they produce. Left uncut, they turn into marrows.

Generally, courgettes have a deep green skin with pale firm flesh, but some varieties are bright yellow, or very light green, or striped.

To cut courgettes from their stems, use a sharp knife and leave about 1 inch (3 cm) of stem with the vegetable.

To prepare courgettes, wash and dry them. Trim the stalk and flower ends. It is not necessary to peel them if they are sufficiently young and tender.

To freeze, prepare courgettes and cut into slices ¼ inch (1 cm) thick. Blanch in boiling water for 1 minute, then plunge them into cold water (to stop them cooking). Pat them dry with paper towels, place them in plastic bags or containers and freeze them. They will keep for up to 6 months.

Grate fresh courgettes when they are plentiful in the garden and store in recipe-size portions in freezer containers.

You may achieve an attractive effect by peeling courgettes with a potato peeler, leaving alternate strips of green skin and white flesh.

Courgettes are most loved of all squashes because of their versatility and ease of cooking. They may be steamed or boiled, sautéed in butter, dipped in egg and breadcrumbs and fried, grilled, roasted, or stuffed and baked.

For easy roasting, just place courgettes in an ovenproof dish, sprinkle with crushed garlic, broken basil leaves and olive oil. Then bake in a hot oven until tender, turning slices from time to time.

Grilled zucchini is an ideal vegetable to cook on the outdoor grill over hot coals.

Baby courgettes have no seeds or pith and have flesh that is completely firm. Use small firm courgettes whenever possible, no longer than 6 inches, with a healthy looking shiny skin, as these have more flavor.

Baby courgettes need little or no cooking. Just steam them whole or blanch them. Larger courgettes can be sliced and steamed or boiled with care taken that they are not overcooked and soggy.

Courgettes are usually sliced into rounds. If they are to be stuffed, cut them into half lengthways. Spoon out seeds and flesh without piercing skin and leaving at least ½ inch (1 cm) flesh.

Although courgettes come in a huge range of shapes, sizes, and colors, they have in common their flavor, which is almost exactly the same regardless of appearance.

Marrows are simply overgrown courgettes, but not as firm or as tasteful when cooked.

Vegetable marrow was not introduced to England until the nineteenth century, when it became known, with Mrs. Beeton giving several recipes for it.

Marrows, and all squashes, were a staple food of native American Indians, eaten traditionally with corn and beans. The three vegetables symbolize three inseparable sisters in an Iroquois myth.

Courgette blossoms, seldom found in shops, may be carefully removed (after waiting for the plants to pollinate) and frozen until enough flowers are collected to cook, perhaps in Courgette Blossom Soup.

Fragile, rich, yellow courgette flowers can be dipped in batter and fried to light golden fritters. However, make all the preparations before picking the flowers as they wilt rapidly.

Recent increased demand for the flowers has resulted in the breeding of courgette plants solely for their flowers with consequent production of tiny baby courgettes.

Courgettes have a high water content—90%.

Courgettes are rich in potassium and Vitamins A (mostly in the skin), C and folic acid. Keep the skin intact as much as possible, as peeling removes nutrients that are just under the skin as well as valuable fiber.

Like aubergines, courgettes absorb fat readily.

Courgettes are available most of the year and will keep for a week stored in the salad compartment of your refrigerator.

Even Agatha Christie's exotic Belgian detective is interested in discovering the mysterious qualities of courgettes. In *The Murder of Roger Ackroyd* (1926), Hercule Poirot has retired to the village of King's Abbot where he plans to cultivate vegetable marrows.